Information
for Foreigners

Three Plays by Griselda Gambaro

Information
for Foreigners

Three Plays by Griselda Gambaro

Edited, Translated, and with an Introduction
by Marguerite Feitlowitz

With an Afterword by Diana Taylor

Northwestern University Press / Evanston, Illinois

Northwestern University Press
Evanston, Illinois 60208-4170

Portions of "Crisis, Terror, Disappearance: The Theater of Griselda
Gambaro" appeared, in slightly different form, in *Theater,* Summer
1990. An earlier version of scene 9 of *Information for Foreigners*
appeared in *The Literary Review,* Summer 1989. Scene 1 of *Information for Foreigners* appeared in *Bomb,* Summer 1990.

Published 1992 / Printed in the United States of America

10   9   8   7   6   5   4   3

ISBN 0-8101-1033-4

Library of Congress Cataloging in Publication Data will be found
at the end of this book.

∞ The paper used in this publication meets the minimum
requirements of American National Standard for Information
Sciences—Permanence of Paper for Printed Library Materials,
ANSI Z39.48-1992.

Contents

Acknowledgments

For my initial introduction to the work of Griselda Gambaro, I am pleased to cite Kathleen Betsko and Rachel Koenig's *Interviews with Contemporary Women Playwrights* and to thank those editors for giving me Gambaro's address. For their readings of various drafts of these translations, I am grateful to Lynne Alvarez, Shelley Berc, Len Berkman, Donald Futterman, Tom Gruenewald, Alberto Minero, Diana Taylor, and Susana Tubert. *Information for Foreigners* received its first public performance—sixteen years after its composition—at the instigation of Alberto Minero, then director of the theater department at the Americas Society, in New York City. Excerpts were performed subsequently, as the closing to the conference Writing as Political Action: Strategies of Resistance in Latin America, organized by Professor Rose Minc at Montclair State College. *The Walls* was first performed in English at River Arts Repertory, Woodstock, New York, under the direction of Angel Gil y Orrios, whose comments on the translation were invaluable. Melissa Marsland directed the first West Coast production of *The Walls*, at Stark Raving Theatre in Seattle. That production would not have happened save for Martha Gies, who read a story of Gambaro's in *Fiction Network* and resolved to learn more about the author's work. *Antígona Furiosa* had its first performance in English under the auspices of the Women's Project in 1988, as part of the New York International Arts Festival. The director was Valeria Vasilevsky. To all of the artists involved with the above-mentioned productions and workshops—particularly Bill T. Jones and Lawrence Goldhuber—I offer my appreciation.

I am grateful for a Fulbright Research Grant that enabled me to spend six months in Argentina, and for a grant from Theatre Communications Group for my translation of *The Walls*.

I extend special thanks to my husband, David Anderson, who brought his own writerly instincts to close readings of every draft of these translations. His learning, insight, and enthusiasm have nourished this book from the beginning.

For the last five years, I have had the great privilege to work closely with Griselda Gambaro, both in the United States and in Argentina. In every sense she has been a collaborator, welcoming my questions and querying in turn, in detailed discussions of words and images, rhythm and rhyme. Of course she—and everyone here cited—is innocent of any deficiencies in these translations, which are wholly mine.

Crisis, Terror, Disappearance

The Theater of Griselda Gambaro

Life here is surreal

This phrase reverberates in conversations with Griselda Gambaro, one of Argentina's most important and prolific writers. Since 1963, when Gambaro's first book was published, her country has seen five military coups; four other presidents appointed by the army; two blatantly rigged elections; two terms of highly theatrical, fascistic Peronism; several factions of urban guerrillas; and the state-run Dirty War (1976–83), in which some thirty thousand citizens were disappeared, tortured, and murdered.[1] Nineteen eighty-five saw the tempestuous "Trial of the Century," in which the former commanders of the Dirty War were convicted of crimes against humanity: numerous counts of murder, torture, child-stealing, kidnapping, illegal detention, and robbery. On December 29, 1990, these criminals were set free in an unprecedented executive pardon characterized by President Carlos Menem as "necessary for the healing of Argentina, [and] for the rightful restoration of military prestige."[2]

"This is a schizophrenic country," Gambaro once told me, "a country that lives two lives. The courteous and generous have their counterpart in the violent and the armed who move among the shadows—para-military police units that weren't dissolved at the end of the Dirty War, secret services that still operate, all blatantly serving totalitarian interests. One never really knows what country one is living in, because the two co-exist. . . . Argentina is seismic as well as schizophrenic. From night to day, things can change drastically owing to causes below the surface, behind the screen that's offered up as reality."[3]

Gambaro's work is deeply rooted in Argentina and embodies that country's psychic gestalt. She stayed as long as possible into the Dirty War, somehow enduring menace, terror, and the disappearance of friends and colleagues. Like many Argentine artists and intellectuals, she buried cartons of "suspicious" magazines (including Eduardo Galeano's *Crisis*) in her garden and burned books (such as works by Marx and Freud) that were forbidden. The discovery of such materials by the police would virtually have assured their disappearance. Gambaro was forced into exile in 1977, when one of her novels, *Ganarse la muerte,* was banned by the direct decree of then–de facto president General Jorge Rafael Videla. A banning by the executive was rare— generally censorship was carried out by city hall—and tanta- mount to a death threat. Gambaro lived in Barcelona until 1980; by then the junta was debilitated, and she could return to Argentina. In exile Gambaro wrote a novel, *Dios no nos quiere contentos,* but was unable to write for the theater. For her, a play is "an assemblage of signs, received, modified and given back by the audience."[4] "Exile carries a high price," she said in a recent interview. "In no foreign country—no matter how hospitable— [do] I have the dialogue I have with my compatriots. Our com- mon history means that much can remain tacit; there's no need for exposition or explanation, no need to 'de-code' images and signs."[5]

Owing to their history, Argentines seem preternaturally alert to subtle signs and encoded threats of violence. Gambaro's chief concern has always been violence—its roots, manifestations, and spheres of influence, as well as the ways in which it may be perceived, masked, and denied. Her plays explore the relations between domestic and political violence, repression and complicity, and also the abiding conflations in public life of history and fiction, illusion and substance. She uses blatant artifice in her plays to probe the nature of theatricality and our responses to it, not only in art but also in daily life. In their respective ways, the repressive Church, the military coups, Perón's police state, and the Terror were highly theatrical, indeed ritualized. Their "shows," however, were for real, and the stakes were not just power, but also life and death.

Over the last twenty-five years, Gambaro has deconstructed official policy and practices, exposed tacit developments, and traced the schizoid mood swings of Argentina. Professor Diana Taylor has aptly characterized Gambaro's plays of the 1960s (including *The Walls, The Siamese Twins,* and *In the Country*— also translated as *The Camp*) as "theatre of crisis" and her work of the early 1970s (in particular, *Information for Foreigners*) as "drama of disappearance, obsessed with the 'missing.'"[6] This volume, the first English-language collection of Gambaro's plays, includes one work from each category: *The Walls* and *Information for Foreigners.* The third offering is *Antígona Furiosa,* written in 1985 and 1986, during and shortly after the trial of the Dirty War commanders.

Gambaro is one of the most widely produced playwrights in Latin America. Eastern and Western Europe are also staunch supporters of her work. In the United States she has had relatively few productions, as this goes to press. Here, her work has been taught, written about, and discussed primarily in academic and literary circles. Gambaro's writing does not conform to the expectations that many in the United States bring to literature from Latin America. It is not imbued with magic realism, nor does it partake of the *costumbrista* tradition. Gambaro's theater has sometimes been called absurdist. This is a misapprehension. As Gambaro has said, her plays derive from a thoroughly Argentine genre, *el grotesco,* or grotesque, which goes back to Armando Discépolo (1887–1971). Gambaro's work is not metaphysical in the way of European absurdism; it does not focus on states of being. It is combative theater, and it grows out of the belief that the human condition can change.

If I had to choose one word to describe Gambaro's writing, it would be *prismatic*. Her chief artistic strategies are blatant artifice, a deep embedding of cultural codes (a not unusual recourse among writers who have had to deal with censorship), and "collages" made with appropriated material together with her own language. Other devices include irony, parody, allusion, and black comedy. By the ways in which she juxtaposes and frames violent acts, Gambaro divests them of any aesthetic or erotic "allure." Without stripping repressors of the danger they present, she avoids the torturer-as-most-fascinating-character pitfall through demystification, buffoonery, and ridicule. Gambaro gets her message across by not focusing on the "humanity" of torturers: a liking for dogs, music, or children does not entitle them to our respectful attention.

Sunday I'm going to the country

Although *The Walls* forecasts the era of the *desaparecidos,* it deals not on the political level, but on a universal mythic plane. The plot is easily summarized: the Young Man is abducted upon returning home from a day in the country—ostensibly because it is thought he may be a character in a particular novel—and brought to a luxurious, 1850s-style room (although the time is the present). On the wall is a period portrait of a tranquil young man gazing out a window. The lovely curtains in the Young Man's room are found to cover not a window but a bare wall. Though not a cell in the conventional sense, the room is a prison. From time to time, anguished screams reverberate offstage. The Young Man's keepers (an Usher and a Functionary) explain, "The walls are falling in on somebody." The Young Man does not believe it. He is innocent, he continually reminds himself, ergo they will set him free. But there are no reliable ergos in this world, no identifiable logic or cause-and-effect. With lights going on and off at random, day and night become untrustworthy fictions. The Young Man's room gradually shrinks, as the walls close in. The curtains and various appointments—notably the painting—begin to vanish, foreshadowing the Young Man's own disappearance. When finally the Usher tells him that at midnight the walls will fall in on him, crushing him to death, the Young Man still does not believe it. He is totally disoriented by crisis, by the crisis happening to him. Like a resistant viewer of a play, he cannot suspend his disbelief. "Sunday I'm going to the country," he tells himself over and over, calming himself with a deceptive fiction.

The Walls explores art-as-truth and art-as-fiction and the ways in which art, specifically theatricality, can be used either to alert us to or distract us from crisis. The set Gambaro conceived—in reality, a death set—is beautiful, refined, "artistic." Midway through the play, the Usher produces a hideously kitschy porcelain doll belonging to the Young Man's landlady.[7] The Young

Man admits he hates the vile-looking thing and has felt oppressed by it in the past, but when the Functionary tells him he is free to smash it, he cannot. The Functionary says, "Art is all that deserves to last—lofty sentiments, things and beings coming to life. You haven't smashed the doll so as to assure that there will be beauty in the world, order. In a word: so the trees can keep growing and putting forth new leaves, so the earth does not become a desolate wasteland." Later, after beating up the Young Man, the Usher says, "You've got to understand me! My great yearning to return to the country, to a healthy, bucolic life, often drives me to actions not exactly in good taste, even a little contemptible, I admit. But is it my fault? . . . I commit contemptible acts under the influence of lyrical needs. Don't I deserve some tolerance?"

Once as we discussed this work, Gambaro remarked, "Onstage the crisis is very obvious, the consequences—for one who's willing to see them—are clear. What's mysterious is the climate, or system, offstage. This reflects the time in which *The Walls* was written. Today, the situation is reversed. If we consider Argentina as a theatric phenomenon, and I do, the system 'offstage' has been demystified. We know the workings of its double discourse very well. Today what is unclear are the consequences. From one moment to the next, we really don't know what is going to happen to us."

> *The repression is directed against a minority we do*
> *not consider Argentine . . . those whose* ideas *are*
> *contrary to our Western, Christian civilization.*—De
> facto president General Jorge Rafael Videla, 1976

Technically groundbreaking and virtuosic, *Information for Foreigners* is a masterpiece. Written in the period 1971–73, the play prophetically foretold an era of government-sponsored terrorism not only against persons whose activities were deemed subversive but also against those whose thoughts were grounds for kidnapping, torture, and death. Gambaro hid the play in her house, then smuggled it out when she fled into exile. For years, the play circulated in samizdat among theater people in Europe, but when companies offered productions, Gambaro refused permission, fearing repercussions against family members still in

Argentina. An early version appeared in a small Italian theater journal. A couple of articles were published in *Latin American Theatre Review.*[8] Then there was intercontinental word-of-mouth. The translation in this volume was begun in 1986, from a then-unpublished, revised manuscript. *Información para extranjeros* was published in Buenos Aires in 1987, in the second of five volumes of Gambaro's collected plays, but it has not been produced there, nor are the prospects very good.[9] Its only performances have been at English-language workshops and readings in the United States.

Gambaro has described *Information* as a "guided tour of the places of repression and indignity." The piece should be performed in a house or warehouse, calling up the spaces used for detention and torture. The audience is split into groups, and a Guide leads each group from scene to scene. The Guides are by turn charming, unctuous, and ambiguous. They basically are untrustworthy characters on whom we nevertheless must depend, whom we nevertheless must follow from scene to scene through narrow, often darkened passageways (sometimes they get lost). Gambaro makes clear that audience members are not to be endangered or made to participate in the action, though it is conceivable that some might question, resist, or object to what is being shown. The setup raises questions about the implications of confinement and confusion and the significance of leading, following, and bearing witness.

The title of the play alludes, not particularly to non-Argentines, but to those Argentines who even in 1973 persisted in ignoring information about the horrible events of the previous two years. "Explanation: For Foreigners," the Guides say, as they introduce their deadpan readings of newspaper articles that appeared in the Argentine press in 1971–72. Many of these pieces were later found to be false and/or incomplete. Stage action sometimes parallels the report, sometimes renders it with black humor, and sometimes treats it in a Grand Guignol manner. To put it in musical terms, the stage business is always in a different key than the article.

Information for Foreigners is a play that hinges on juxtaposition: children's games with scenes of torture, a trumped-up arrest with *Othello,* the poetry of victims of the Dirty War with the Milgram experiment.[10] Gambaro uses the traditional Argentine games of Martin Fisherman and Anton Pirulero—both about arbitrary reward and punishment—to point up the differences between adult and infantile violence. (Gambaro's view is that children's violence generally is not criminal, whereas that of adults most certainly is.) Theatrically, the games intensify the images of adult violence. They provoke anxiety on another level as well, though, for the games are an integral part of an audience's shared culture and do contain threats (play along, or suffer the blame), roughness, and scapegoating. The spectator is forced to ask, What are the relations, the refinements, the trajectories between "innocent" and "guilty" violence in the life of an individual? In the life of a nation? As Gambaro has written, "Everything in this play happens through theatricality, or artifice. That is to say, through a cover, or wrapping, that transcends the action itself, but nonetheless leaves the meaning intact. The work must be 'acted,' 'represented,' 'disguised.' Only this will make it tolerable; otherwise no one would have the strength to watch."[11]

A good deal of the appropriated material in this play comes from the theater. In scene 17, a rehearsal of *Othello* refers to the Grupo 67 theater company's arrest on trumped-up drug charges and subsequent illegal imprisonment. Another female prisoner, apparently an actress, repeatedly sings snatches of the lullabye from scene 2 of Federico García Lorca's *Blood Wedding*. In scene 19, the Guard sings a few lines from one of García Lorca's puppet plays, *Los títeres de cachiporra*. Surely these appropriations call attention to the fact that theater artists are particularly vulnerable during repressive regimes (García Lorca, we are reminded, was murdered by Spanish fascists). They also add yet another level of theatricality to stage business about "real," yet highly theatrical, goings-on. That the line between "reality" and "theater" can be manipulated is pointed up in scene 17, when Actor #2 involuntarily slips into character with the arresting policeman, as though the two were rehearsing *Othello*. The words being spoken are Shakespeare's, but the arrest—however unreal it may seem to Actor #2—is hardly fictional. Theater, as we are shown, can be put to nefarious uses. There is a particularly chilling reminder of this in the lines "violín, violón / es la mejor razón." The couplet refers to the reign of caudillo Juan Manuel de Rosas (1829–52), who had violin music played during the decapitations of his enemies.[12]

Information for Foreigners presents extraordinary challenges to the translator. The work embraces poetry and prose, as well as dramatic writing. There are scores of distinct voices, multiple levels of diction, and references and echoes between texts, places, and historical eras. In addition to Gambaro's language, lines need to be translated from García Lorca, as well as Garcilaso de la Vega (1501–36), contemporary Argentine poet Juan Gelman, and Marina, a young Greek writer who was disappeared. *Information* was unlike any translation I had previously done. My linguistic sources—beyond the original text, the author, dictionaries, and lexicons—were unexpected. Indispensable was *Nunca más: The Report of the Argentine National Commission on the Disappeared.*[13] Apart from its exhaustive information, I needed this book for its language. For there developed during the Dirty War an argot of dissimulation in which familiar, domestic expressions carried sinister, even deadly, implications. Today in Argentina certain words still bear the scars of having been twisted by the Dirty War repressors. The meanings of key words are encoded: *security,* for example, really means repression: *order* translates as terror; *pardon* signifies praise. This lends a crucial layer of meaning, an additional layer of translation (even for native Argentines reading the original), to the following Tin Pan Alley song from scene 12:

> Peace and security
> That is our domain
> With a little authority
> Order will be maintained!

Christopher Middleton has described translation "as a species of mime."[14] This analogy is particularly apt in regard to *Information for Foreigners*. A mime works in space, creating structures in the air, playing against and in these structures with his or her body. So, too, in *Information,* much of the meaning derives from, is framed by, and is expressed through the space in which it is performed. Perhaps most important, at a performance of this piece, everyone, wittingly or unwittingly, is in some sense a mime.

The living are the great sepulchre of the dead

For obvious reasons, Antigone is a common theme among Latin American playwrights. Gambaro's *Antígona Furiosa,* however, is distinctive: rather than pitting a bad government against a good populace, it deals with passivity in the face of repression, popular compliance with terror. Quoted by the Chorus is the old Argentine saying, "Punishment always presupposes crime, my girl. There are no innocents." Antígona is mocked and reviled by the Chorus, comprising two *porteños* sitting at a Buenos Aires café. Except for the café table, the set consists of Antígona's cell, a huge, pyramidal, iron-barred cage. The first image is that of Antígona hanged. Having refused a last bowl of water, she declares, "Mouth moist with my own saliva, I will go to my death. Proudly."

In Laura Yusem's original Buenos Aires production, Antígona was played by Bettina Muraña, a *mestiza* dancer. "Our work was far from naturalistic," Yusem told me. "It was a form of dance-theater in which light and the particulars of the space were of capital importance. Certain sequences were ritualistic." Creon was represented by a movable pectoral made of painted polyester (torso, helmet, arms) used in various ways by the actors in the Chorus—worn like a garment, held like a shield, manipulated like a puppet.

Though the slang and intonations are *porteño,* there are no explicit references to the Mothers of the Plaza de Mayo, nor to any specific aspect of the Dirty War. The language, which incorporates quotes and echoes from Sophocles, Shakespeare, and Rubén Darío, extends beyond Argentina, not only inscribing the country's history into that of the world but also forcefully asserting that *Antígona* was not just happening there and then but is happening, everywhere, always.

I return to Middleton's notion that translation is "a species of mime" and wonder if the analogy might be extended to the reading of texts intended to be acted. In the present collection, metaphors of movement and travel—and conversely, obstruction and confinement—abound. Space and the ways in which we occupy it become central concerns. Reading itself is a form of transport; like space, a text must be negotiated. Great anxiety attaches to not being able to move through space; it is also agonizing to witness, or envision, another's imprisonment. For the Young Man in *The Walls* this anxiety becomes all-encompassing as the space around him shrinks, closes in for the kill. For him and for us—as readers, as witnesses—there is paralyzing terror in not knowing the mechanisms of this disaster, which operate from a diabolical space beyond, offstage. The transition from *The Walls* to *Information* is not easy to navigate. We go from being witnesses of a hostile environment to inhabitants, however temporary, of a hellish one. Now where are the boundaries between onstage and off? Who, really, is providing the spectacle? Those performing, or those who lend their eyes? At the end, as we exit the text—leave the space— a police siren goes off, its sudden, harrowing wail piercing a last refrain of poetry, causing us—on the threshold of . . . what?—to panic. By the time we arrive at *Antígona Furiosa,* which plays in the round, we have become "the walls." Or have we? Gambaro's plays call upon us to reflect, decide, act.

Marguerite Feitlowitz

Notes

1. Though figures vary, thirty thousand *desaparecidos,* given by the Mothers of the Plaza de Mayo, has the greatest currency in Argentine human rights circles.

2. Responding to one hundred thousand protesters, President Menem said, "You can present me with a million marches, the decision to pardon has already been made." ("Me pueden hacer un millón de marchas, pero la decisión de indultar ya está tomada.") New York's *El Diario / La Prensa,* October 1, 1989.

3. Gambaro, interview by Feitlowitz, in "Two Argentine Writers," *Bomb,* no. 32 (Summer 1990): 54.

4. From remarks made at Writing as Political Action: Strategies of Resistance in Latin America, a conference sponsored by Montclair State College, Upper Montclair, N.J., October 1987.

5. "Two Argentine Writers," 54.

6. Diana Taylor, *Theatre of Crisis: Drama and Politics in Latin America* (Lexington: University Press of Kentucky, 1991), 98.

7. Ibid., 96–147. Taylor offers a penetrating discussion on the role of kitsch in fascism.

8. Dick Gerdes, "Recent Argentine Vanguard Theatre: Gambaro's *Información para extranjeros," Latin American Theatre Review* 11, no. 2 (Spring 1978): 11–16; Rosalea Postma, "Space and Spectator in the Theatre of Griselda Gambaro: *Información para extranjeros," Latin American Theatre Review* 13, no. 1 (Fall 1980): 35–45.

9. Gambaro's collected plays are published in Buenos Aires by Ediciones de la Flor.

10. The Milgram experiment was first done in the 1960s under the auspices of the Yale University psychology department. Subsequently it was performed at other U.S. universities and in Munich. Under the guise of investigating the role of punishment in learning, it tested individuals' willingness to inflict pain—even death—on strangers. A designated "pupil" was made to answer memory word-matching questions; if the pupil answered wrong, the "teacher" was authorized to give him or her a certain voltage of electricity. With every error, the voltage increased. Unbeknownst to the teacher, the electricity and the pupil's agonized screams were faked. In Germany, 85 percent of the subjects shocked their pupils to "death"; in the United States, 66 percent did. See Stanley Milgram, *Obedience to Authority* (New York: Harper and Row, 1974).

11. Personal correspondence, Gambaro to Feitlowitz, March 28, 1986. "Lo que sucede es que todo eso que pasa en la obra, pasa o debe pasar a través de la teatralidad, del artificio. Es decir, de una envoltura que transcienda el hecho en sí, dejándolo intacto en su sentido, sin embargo. . . . Por más terrible que sea la obra, debe ser 'actuada,' 'representada,' 'disfrazada.' Esto es lo que debe hacerla soportable (sino nadie tendría fuerzas para verla) y para los actores debe hacerla también gratificante. Tú sabes, como siempre, placer y dolor." The last part, not translated in the body of this essay, reads: "And for the actors this should also make it gratifying. You know, as always, pleasure and pain."

12. Because these lines required a gloss to signify in English, I devised a substitute, with the author's approval. The couplet appears on p. 112 of the de la Flor edition.

13. *Nunca más: The Report of the Argentine National Commission on the Disappeared* (New York: Farrar, Straus, Giroux, 1986).

14. Christopher Middleton, "Translation as a Species of Mime," *Translation* 17 (Fall 1986): 215–24.

The Walls

Characters

Young Man
Usher
Functionary

The Walls (written in 1963) premiered on April 11, 1966, at the Teatro Agón in Buenos Aires, with the following cast and artistic crew:

YOUNG MAN	Francisco Cocuzza
USHER	Natalio Oxman
FUNCTIONARY	Rafael Pollio
SET AND COSTUMES	Luis Diego Pedreira
MISE-EN-SCENE AND	
DIRECTION	José María Paolantonio

Act 1

Scene 1

A bedroom in the style of the 1850s, very comfortable, practically luxurious. Heavy curtains on the left wall hide what seems to be a window; in the center of the rear wall, a large painting with a magnificent carved frame represents, with the *verismo* of the period, a languid young man looking out a window. A single door leads to other parts of the house.

The curtain rises. A timid and kindly seeming YOUNG MAN, beautifully dressed in late nineteenth-century style, is seated in a Viennese-type chair next to the door, apparently waiting for someone. At his side stands an USHER, unmoving, in a simple uniform buttoned to his neck. The neatness of the uniform contrasts with the USHER's beard, patchy after several days' growth.

A long silence.

Suddenly, from elsewhere in the house, we hear a scream for help. The scream ends in a stifled howl.

The YOUNG MAN leaps up.

YOUNG MAN: Did you hear?

USHER: (natural, affirmative) Mmm-hmm.

YOUNG MAN: What was it?

USHER: A scream. (smiling) The walls fell in on somebody.

YOUNG MAN: Somebody was screaming, asking for help.

USHER: Really? Don't believe it. The acoustics. Inferior construction, half-baked bricks. Negligence. A shame, but we can't tear the house down because of it.

YOUNG MAN: It was a person, a voice.

USHER: (surprised) Whose?

YOUNG MAN: Somebody's. I don't know.

USHER: (paternal) You're dreaming. (He cocks an ear.) Did you hear that?

YOUNG MAN: (listens, then) No. Nothing.

USHER: How your senses deceive you! I cocked an ear, and when I did, the ear drum thundered like an orchestra. Bom! Bom! Habit.

YOUNG MAN: But before, before I *did* hear a scream, a cry for help. Somebody seemed . . . about to surrender his soul.

USHER: (amused) I never heard it expressed that way! We say liquidated, dead. Also, finished. But "surrender his soul" . . . that's beautiful, poetic. Are you a writer?

YOUNG MAN: No.

USHER: It's a pity. You have a gift. Why don't you sit down?

YOUNG MAN: That scream made my hair stand on end.

USHER: Calm down. Outside of that, you never hear anything here. Total silence. I don't know if you'll like it. Sometimes it's boring. Other times, I admit, it calms the nerves. Are you nervous?

YOUNG MAN: (sits, nervous) No.

USHER: Well, you should be.

YOUNG MAN: You think . . . ?

USHER: Without a doubt.

YOUNG MAN: Then there is reason to worry!

USHER: None. But it's always good to prime the nerves. You don't want to go slack.

YOUNG MAN: Well, if I'm to talk with you sincerely, I can't deny that I am worried by this situation, I don't under-stand . . .

USHER: (interrupting) What situation? You're mistaken. No chain of events created anything. You're endowing events with guilty intentions. No, no, the events are innocent. Quite simply, you arrived here, and we thank you for being so gracious—to converse with us a little.

YOUNG MAN: They brought me.

USHER: Who? Don't tell me the tall one and the small one "brought you."

YOUNG MAN: But they did. "Come with us," they said.

USHER: That's different! What a muddled young man you are!

YOUNG MAN: Me?

USHER: Yes, you. You get things all tangled up. It isn't right.

YOUNG MAN: I only said that they brought me here. (tries to smile) I wouldn't have come alone.

USHER: Hah! Look at that! You could say they did you a favor. You couldn't have come alone.

YOUNG MAN: I don't understand. They made me!

USHER: Why would they make you? In any case, it's not so clear. Did they chain you? Did they drag you by the hair? No. They invited you. Politely. I know them. You agreed: with your own legs you climbed into the car; with your own eyes you saw the route; your own ass, pardon the expression, sat itself down on that seat. (The YOUNG MAN stands up.) No, remain seated.

YOUNG MAN: (stupidly thinking he might have refused) But could I have stayed there? Could I have said no and gone home?

USHER: (amused) No! No, you couldn't have done that! (laughs) No way, impossible!

YOUNG MAN: (perplexed) Then . . . you admit there was a certain amount of pressure, right?

USHER: It comes to the same thing! What stubbornness! No, no. We don't force anyone. And another thing, we're not exactly the plague! I'm not saying our social graces are perfect, but to say one only arrives here in chains . . . It's not very polite.

YOUNG MAN: No, sir! What are you saying? You're changing what I meant. That is, I would have preferred another chance. I'd spent the day outside, in the country.

USHER: Relaxing.

YOUNG MAN: Relaxing, of course, but I walked among the trees, I went rowing. I'm not used to that much exercise, so . . .

USHER: (exultant) You should have told me before! What a mixed-up way to talk, neither of us understanding the other! I congratulate you!

YOUNG MAN: Me? What for?

USHER: You spent the day in the country! You're like me! I adore the country, the pastures, the animals! Ah, and the sunsets? Tell me about the sunsets? (pop-eyed) The clouds and the trees! The songs of the birds!

(There's a knock at the door.)

VOICE OF THE FUNCTIONARY: Am I interrupting? Can I come in?

(The FUNCTIONARY, a tall, robust, middle-aged gentleman, enters. He is dressed with loud elegance, the color of his vest too bright, the whiteness and embroidery of his shirt excessive. His face is nice and jovial, his gestures theatrical and emphatic, his laugh easy.)

FUNCTIONARY: My good man! How are you? For a long time now I have wished to meet you. You know the saying, "seize opportunity by the forelock." That's what I'm doing! Very, very pleased to see you! (Warmly shakes the YOUNG MAN's hand. Moves away, scrutinizes him.) You're just as I imagined you. Young, obliging, an open face, loyal beyond all doubt. Am I wrong? (doesn't wait for an answer) No, no! I know! I hope you'll excuse me for the slight change we made in your plans. You had plans, didn't you? There isn't a young man alive who doesn't dream of some enchanting young girl. When the sunset's thrilling, the body's willing, eh? (a short, complicitous laugh) Well, everything will turn out for the best. *Tutto per bene,* right? You can leave, Usher. I'll talk with the young man. Young people speak my language. (amused) I speak none! (He laughs. The USHER exits. The YOUNG MAN, who hasn't had a chance to say a word, doesn't know what to say now. He takes a few steps, looking anxiously at the FUNCTIONARY. The FUNCTIONARY imitates the YOUNG MAN's expression, returning his gaze and smiling with encouraging cordiality. He laughs. Finally, looking around, he asks.) The room . . . is to your liking? What a place, eh? In all honesty, you weren't expecting this surprise.

YOUNG MAN: No.

FUNCTIONARY: (jubilantly) Ah! Finally I hear your voice! Congratulations! (He presses the YOUNG MAN's hands.) Beautiful voice, excellently modulated. Again, again, once more! Do you like the room?

YOUNG MAN: Yes.

FUNCTIONARY: "No, yes." Very good! (He hugs him.) Very good, I repeat! I took special care, pains worthy of a better cause, so that your lodging should be comfortable. I sold my soul.

YOUNG MAN: Please, you shouldn't have bothered.

FUNCTIONARY: But it wasn't any bother! The results are their own reward. This isn't a princely lodging, unfortunately.

YOUNG MAN: Still . . .

FUNCTIONARY: (cutting him off) Still, it could be the room of a young man in comfortable circumstances. Somebody who's free and easy, who has no troubles. Evidently, not your case.

YOUNG MAN: Am I in trouble?

FUNCTIONARY: (smiles) Who isn't in trouble? Tell me: at home do you enjoy such comfort, such curtains, such furniture? Did you have this much space for stretching your legs?

YOUNG MAN: By no means. My room is much more modest. I live well, but without luxuries.

FUNCTIONARY: I'm happy to hear it—your sincerity, I mean. (He points to the painting.) Did you see the painting? We hung it yesterday. I searched in the basement for a pleasing subject: youth, nostalgia . . . Did you notice the fine execution, the subtleties?

YOUNG MAN: Yes.

FUNCTIONARY: But talk a little! I seem a chatterbox. (alarmed) Do I, perhaps, intimidate you? Oh, my feelings would be very hurt.

YOUNG MAN: (with effort conquers his timidity) No, no, sir. I was expecting to find a . . . (hesitates)

FUNCTIONARY: Yes, don't be afraid!

YOUNG MAN: (timidly) A cell . . .

FUNCTIONARY: (marveling) A cell! (laughs) You're joking! The ideas people have . . .

YOUNG MAN: And I find myself with this room . . . Yes, much more comfortable than my own.

FUNCTIONARY: What an idea . . .

YOUNG MAN: I thought about the sky framed in a tiny square. I was afraid.

FUNCTIONARY: What were you afraid of?

YOUNG MAN: Well, just that—a cell. Being confined, unable to open a door and go out.

FUNCTIONARY: (marveling) You're so far from reality!

YOUNG MAN: This big window, these curtains surprise me. May I?

FUNCTIONARY: Yes, of course.

YOUNG MAN: Mentally, I had prepared myself for bars, the conventional sign of a ce . . . (He parts the drapes. They open on a plain wall.)

FUNCTIONARY: (laughs, pleased) What a stroke! What a stroke! (The YOUNG MAN, astounded, turns back toward him.) My idea, element of surprise. Curtains that don't cover a window are transformed into pure symbols of well-being, of luxury. Do you realize? I avoid all utilitarian waste. (The YOUNG MAN is silent.) What's the matter? Did I say something wrong?

YOUNG MAN: (hesitating) I don't know, I really . . .

FUNCTIONARY: (sour) What?

YOUNG MAN: (listless) It hadn't occurred to me. It's a . . . particular . . . point of view.

FUNCTIONARY: Logical. My own. Might there be another?

YOUNG MAN: I thought I'd find a window there . . .

FUNCTIONARY: You would have preferred it?

YOUNG MAN: Maybe . . .

FUNCTIONARY: (laughs, paternally) What a child you are.

YOUNG MAN: Would a question inconvenience you?

FUNCTIONARY: As many as you like! That's why I'm here.

YOUNG MAN: If there were a window there . . . would it have bars?

FUNCTIONARY: (with sincere and amused surprise) Bars? What an idea! *Quelle idée!* What for?

YOUNG MAN: Well . . . if this were a cell, it wouldn't be so crazy . . .

FUNCTIONARY: (offended) A cell? You have an *idée fixe!* With such luxury, with such *confort?* Come on, it's like a wonderland.

YOUNG MAN: Excuse me. I don't know why they brought me, (corrects himself) why I ended up here.

FUNCTIONARY: (shrugs) And if you don't know, how should I know?

YOUNG MAN: I came, but they invited me.

FUNCTIONARY: They? Who?

YOUNG MAN: The . . . "the tall one and the small one," the Usher called them. One was tall, and the other, small.

FUNCTIONARY: That's right. I sent them.

YOUNG MAN: (with a smile of relief) You!

FUNCTIONARY: Yes, but still it's a little mindless of you to arrive here and not know the reason.

YOUNG MAN: It was night. I was worn out after a day in the country. They seemed . . . strong, powerful. Maybe it's dumb . . . but they appeared to be armed.

FUNCTIONARY: (alarmed) Holy God! Don't tell me they . . . ?

YOUNG MAN: No, no. They didn't threaten me with guns. They asked my name under the light in the station. Then I saw the bulges in their pockets, they kept their hands in their pockets, I had the impression . . .

FUNCTIONARY: (very annoyed) Impressions! I too have my hand in my pocket. (takes his open hand out of his pocket) So what?

YOUNG MAN: You're right. Now that I'm thinking about it calmly, maybe I acted badly. My fatigue got the better of me.

FUNCTIONARY: (indifferent) Or the night. Or the two men. Or the guns they had in their pockets. It's all possible.

YOUNG MAN: All I did was follow them. "Come with us and you'll know the reason," they said.

FUNCTIONARY: Of course, you came for a reason. That much is clear.

YOUNG MAN: (disoriented) Yes.

FUNCTIONARY: Well, you shouldn't have, my good man! Why did you?

YOUNG MAN: Then . . . I can go?

FUNCTIONARY: (laughs) Ah, what a child you are! Not now. There's a reason. Whom did you talk to? Tell me everything. I'm your father.

YOUNG MAN: The Usher received me at the door, led me to this room.

FUNCTIONARY: (furious at the omission) This princely room! It's not a dump! (as the YOUNG MAN, struck dumb, looks at him open-mouthed) Go on!

YOUNG MAN: I sat here, to wait.

FUNCTIONARY: (concerned) The Usher offered you a seat, didn't he?

YOUNG MAN: Yes.

FUNCTIONARY: (calmed) He's very nice. You'll see for yourself. But I interrupt. Go on.

YOUNG MAN: We heard a scream. Somebody was screaming.

FUNCTIONARY: (smiling) Didn't make you jump, I hope. They're always screaming. It's a vice!

YOUNG MAN: Who?

FUNCTIONARY: The others. They're like you, comfortably lodged, and they scream. The walls fall in on them? (laughs)

YOUNG MAN: That's what the Usher said.

FUNCTIONARY: Uh? What a coincidence! Working so much by my side, he thinks and speaks like I do—mimicry. You know what happens? The excess of comfort makes them inconsiderate, ungrateful. Their character turns sour. They care nothing about the silence, the tranquillity, of others.

YOUNG MAN: I jumped a bit. There was, yes, a lot of silence. What I least expected . . . And besides, it sounded like a scream for help, a truly anguished scream, somebody who— not even at the cost of his life—can believe what is happening to him.

FUNCTIONARY: (smiling) And what was happening? A finger caught in a drawer?

YOUNG MAN: I don't know.

FUNCTIONARY: (irascible) So, the joke's going round, eh? They're relaxing, and they don't like it. So they scream, make a fuss. (He stops being angry and laughs, understandingly.) Ah, youth! Why ask pears of an elm tree? We're not stoic in this country. A little torture and we start screaming to high heaven. Let's not talk about it. Did they explain anything to you about your situation?

YOUNG MAN: No.

FUNCTIONARY: (without listening to him, pleased) Yours is a real situation. The Usher should have told you. You are truly at the turning point . . . Well, what did they tell you? I'll fill in the details.

YOUNG MAN: They didn't tell me anything.

FUNCTIONARY: (indignant) The animal! Those animals! Completely useless. I have to take care of everything. Forgive them, sir. I told them not to explain anything! I could see you all eaten up with worry. What's your name? Ruperto de Hentzau or Hentcau? You must know the story: there's a villain in a novel who's named Ruperto de Hentzau.[1] Better that you're not he.

YOUNG MAN: I'm not.

FUNCTIONARY: Then it couldn't be simpler. You're not?

YOUNG MAN: (smiles) Absolutely not. (reaches into his pocket) I'll show you . . .

FUNCTIONARY: (stops him) I don't need documents! Don't be silly! Your word is enough. (sighs) I'm so glad! That by a twist of fate you might have turned out to be Ruperto de Hentzau—I've been losing sleep. The verification will be delayed a few days. Would it greatly annoy you to stay with us?

YOUNG MAN: I can't. Really, I can't. I work, I have my duties.

FUNCTIONARY: Oh, I know very well that you work and have your duties. I'm informed of things before they happen. In any case, we'll take care of this inconvenience right away. Anything else? (before the YOUNG MAN can speak, good-naturedly) You must realize that on the one hand, sentimental considerations don't count, and that on the other, you won't be able to leave. So: why not stay?

YOUNG MAN: I beg you to consider my job. I'm not sick. What excuse will I give? They're very strict.

FUNCTIONARY: Don't worry about your job. You're young, you'll find another. Or you won't find another. Maybe fate will smile upon you. Did you take a vacation this year? You'll relax for a few days. I'll come every morning to chat with you. We'll have breakfast together. How do you like your coffee? Black, or with milk?

YOUNG MAN: It doesn't matter. Thank you, but for me it's . . .

FUNCTIONARY: (puts his hand on the YOUNG MAN's shoulder) Don't thank me for anything. I feel a little like your father. Let me give you a little advice. Turn a good face to bad times. Even though it wouldn't be right to call this room "bad times." Let's open the curtains. Cut down on the luxury.

(He opens the curtains, then turns back toward the YOUNG MAN.) Did you look at the picture? A first-rate painting. You believed there was a window behind the drapes; I believed there was a window here. (points to the window in the painting) These panes, here, reflect the sun, and like real ones, they're a little dirty. Well, I'm still not convinced . . . Optimism, young man. It's better if there's no window anywhere. I prefer to embellish symbols. Plant windows in a wall, in a painting, in an eye. Everywhere, except in windows. (laughs, observes him) But such sadness, young man! Only death has no remedy. Or death is the remedy. To the contrary. (laughs) Oh, what a head I have! You must be dying of hunger! Did you eat?

YOUNG MAN: No. But I've no appetite, I assure you.

FUNCTIONARY: Well, I'm glad! Why do you have no appetite? Does this happen to you often? Don't be afraid to tell me. It isn't a venereal disease. Have you seen a doctor?

YOUNG MAN: No. Normally I eat a lot, but at the moment . . .

FUNCTIONARY: Because of the situation! Believe me, you can rest in peace. You're not named Ruperto de Hentzau or Hentcau?

YOUNG MAN: By no means. My name is . . .

FUNCTIONARY: I know! Hernández. We just have to verify it so you can go free. Although we can't say you're a prisoner now. This isn't a cell. You must know about cells, about prisons. What filth! What promiscuity! No respect for the human body! Like dogs. (abruptly) What time is it? Would you be so kind? I don't have a watch. You see what poverty?

YOUNG MAN: (takes a watch from his pocket and looks at it. The FUNCTIONARY looks at it avidly.) Eleven-fifteen.

FUNCTIONARY: That late! May I, young man? (He takes the watch and examines it.) Beautiful watch! (returns it) A gift?

YOUNG MAN: Remembrance of my father.

FUNCTIONARY: Ah, fathers, how much we have to thank them for! Is it silver?

YOUNG MAN: Yes, he gave it to me when he died.

FUNCTIONARY: (without thinking of what he's saying) When he died, how nice! Mine gave me nothing. (Again, he takes the watch that the YOUNG MAN is holding in his hands. Points.) Are those his initials?

YOUNG MAN: Yes, I'm named for my father.

FUNCTIONARY: (good-naturedly) Don't say another word! We have to verify it. Matter of routine. (Sorrowfully he returns the watch.) Take it. Where do you keep it?

YOUNG MAN: Here in this pocket. (puts the watch away)

FUNCTIONARY: I'm so tired! Could I sit down on your bed? I say "your bed" because I consider that our guests are the absolute rulers of our rooms. (He sits heavily on the bed, exaggerates.) At my age you can't stay on your feet too long. How I envy your youth! The vigor, the resolve, and—why not say it—your capacities for love. Sit next to me. (The YOUNG MAN sits.) I've had a tiring day. The body takes revenge. The years, fears, tears take on twice their weight. What time did you say it was?

YOUNG MAN: Eleven-fifteen.

FUNCTIONARY: No, it isn't eleven-fifteen. Look.

YOUNG MAN: (takes out the watch. The FUNCTIONARY looks at it again, avidly and with calculation.) Eleven-fifteen . . . a little past.

FUNCTIONARY: (drily) Better to be exact. Eleven-eighteen. Didn't I tell you? Oh yes, yes, life flows into the sea and time goes with it. (laughs) Help me, please. (tries to stand up, exaggerating the effort. The YOUNG MAN helps him solicitously.) Thank you, the joints get stiff, the hinges get rusty. (He gets to his feet, surreptitiously feeling the YOUNG MAN's pockets. After a moment, he seems to recover his agility.) Until tomorrow, son. I'll take care of you. Yes, yes, I'll oil the springs and hinges, pull all the strings. And I'll send the Usher to help you settle in.

YOUNG MAN: Thank you. I don't need anything.

FUNCTIONARY: Don't say that. Every man needs his death, at least. (laughs) Till tomorrow, son, till tomorrow. (He opens

the door and speaks to the USHER, who obviously was waiting behind it.) Go on in, help the gentleman. (to the YOUNG
MAN) The Usher will be entirely at your service. (very paternally) Relax. Sweet dreams! (exits)

USHER: May I, sir? Have you settled in yet?

YOUNG MAN: I had nothing with me. (smiles) I'll manage.

USHER: If you say so. How did it happen?

YOUNG MAN: I was getting off the train, after a day in the
country, and . . .

USHER: (annoyed) The same old story! So that's how you got
here. But you should have thought ahead. To leave without
a change of clothes, some food, enough money! You have
money, don't you?

YOUNG MAN: A little. I never bring much for fear of being
robbed.

USHER: Fine, now you see where excessive fear concerning
money leads, and lack of foresight with all the rest. I don't
know how you're going to manage. The lodgings are comfortable, but you can't demand everything of us.

YOUNG MAN: No, of course not!

USHER: You're a nice young man, I'll say that. I don't see you
trying to take advantage. On the contrary. You'll have to realize, "the Usher is entirely at your service" is poetic license.

YOUNG MAN: I'll try to bother you as little as possible. I was
just going to bed.

USHER: You're like me! So willing! It's a pleasure! Let's shake
on it! Count on me, sir . . . (He pumps his hand effusively.)

YOUNG MAN: Thank you. Everyone here is very kind.

USHER: (drily) No end to kindness. (observes him) You've got a
beard like a billy goat. When did you shave?

YOUNG MAN: (running a hand over his face) This morning. See?
A scratch, I cut myself.

USHER: "This morning," as though the beard didn't grow! It
grows on the dead, what do you expect on the living? A slov-
enly beard is disgusting, don't you think?

YOUNG MAN: But I . . . (runs his hand over his face, vaguely worried) Do I have so much growth?

USHER: See for yourself.

YOUNG MAN: (touches his cheeks) Hardly anything. (The USHER, reproachfully silent, is completely oblivious to his own beard of several days.) Well, can I shave?

USHER: Yes, of course! But how loosely you say "Can I shave?" Sir, one must speak with more judgment. Not ask for things recklessly. What are we supposed to do? We have nothing. We're not a barbershop. Why did you go out without your shaving things?

YOUNG MAN: I went on an outing in the country! This is absurd!

USHER: Is it? Why don't you wake up. Better to sin out of excess than want. Supposing that first thing tomorrow they set you free, you could go directly to the office. But not with that stubble. Out of the question.

YOUNG MAN: The Functionary said "a few days."

USHER: A few days, what for? To verify if you're Hentcau or Hentzau? Come on, they'll know tonight.

YOUNG MAN: Then I can go?

USHER: Not tonight, no. They never let anyone go at night. 'Cause of the robbers, the darkness. First thing tomorrow, yes.

YOUNG MAN: Then I could make it on time.

USHER: That would be great. (understanding) Do they dislike you?

YOUNG MAN: At the office? No, no, they like me. But I prefer not to change the rhythm of things. (Again he rubs his face.) Could you help me? I would really appreciate it.

USHER: Wonderful. In what way?

YOUNG MAN: (not understanding) What do you mean?

USHER: In what way will you . . . how shall I say . . . well, never mind. Appreciation has so many forms. But the problem of shaving things, how do we solve that? You'll have to buy soap, a razor, a good cream . . .

YOUNG MAN: Without cream is fine . . .

USHER: Don't believe it, the skin suffers. Come on, I can't stay here indefinitely. (extends his hand) What will it be?

YOUNG MAN: (takes out his wallet, counts the bills, and with visible regret removes one) Is that enough?

USHER: (takes it, impertinently) What about the soap? Or are you thinking of shaving without soap, my shining knight? I already told you that we lack everything here. We've had little opportunity to serve young men as peculiar as yourself.

YOUNG MAN: As myself? I don't understand.

USHER: Yes, young men who think of shaving before . . . (heavily significant silence)

YOUNG MAN: (turns pale) Before? You said "before." Before what?

USHER: (a stupid smile) I said "before"? How strange! It's a word I never use: I have a grudge against it. To clarify *before,* I say *after.* My actions always trail behind me, with a certain delay. "After taking a nap," I say, "I'm going for a walk."

YOUNG MAN: (low) You said "before."

USHER: (as though he didn't understand) No, no. I never go before. I lie down, sleep a while, and, afterward, go for a walk—lucid, fit to kill. By fracturing time, I reconcile language with my actions. Some words I despise. Others avoid me of their own accord. I assure you that I had banished it from my vocabulary, but it must have come back.

YOUNG MAN: You said it. Why?

USHER: I don't remember! Is it that you too want to say it?

YOUNG MAN: No. But why did you say it? Before *what?*

USHER: Drop the subject, will you? It's very boring. When do you want the soap for shaving, tomorrow?

YOUNG MAN: Now, if possible.

USHER: Fine. Did you see how you said "if possible" and I asked you no questions? (He shows the YOUNG MAN the money.) This won't suffice. If I could buy on credit, I would, but I can't even for you—they know me. What a time to shave!

YOUNG MAN: (holds out a second bill) How's that? Is it enough?

USHER: (impertinent, with his hand open) No. It's not. (When the YOUNG MAN adds another bill, he closes his hand and pockets the money. Very amiably.) I'll be back in two minutes. Try not to get bored. You can pace around the room, enjoy the painting, look out the window. You'll see a young man looking out the window. Sleep a little. I'll be right back!

(He exits. After a moment, the YOUNG MAN tries the lock. The door is locked from the outside. He returns to the center of the room, raps his knuckles on a piece of furniture to gauge its solidity, and contemplates the painting with ingenuous admiration. Then he takes off his shoes and lies down. A noise is heard outside. The YOUNG MAN gets up, walks to the door, and tries the lock. It doesn't give. With a gesture of surprise and discouragement, he again lies down, careful not to wrinkle his clothes. The set grows dim.)

YOUNG MAN: (falling asleep) As soon as the Usher arrives, I'll shave. Yes, I'll shave and tomorrow . . . tomorrow, first thing . . .

(Again there is a scream from elsewhere in the house. An intense light illumines the room. The YOUNG MAN sits bolt upright in bed. Darkness.)

Scene 2

As the lights come up, there are several violent knocks at the door.

VOICE OF THE USHER: (yelling) Young man, young man, open! Wake up!

(The YOUNG MAN wakes with a violent start. Instinctively he starts running toward the door, but then stops, uncertain, for now all is silent. He goes to the door and tries the lock. It doesn't give. He stammers.)

YOUNG MAN: It's locked . . .

VOICE OF THE USHER: (sweetly) Open up, young man, I pray you.

YOUNG MAN: It's locked!

VOICE OF THE USHER: Your food is getting cold, and it's a shame. This hallway is full of drafts. Do you want me to catch cold? You devil! Open, please. Come on, do me a favor. Take one step, now another . . . put your hand on the latch, now open!

(In spite of himself, the YOUNG MAN has followed the instructions. He tries the lock: it doesn't give. He backs away, discouraged, uncomprehending.)

YOUNG MAN: I . . . I can't open! The door is locked!

VOICE OF THE USHER: (impatient) Come on! You've gone too far! Who gave you so much confidence, boy? Not me. Don't answer! You'll pay for this! Open up! (The USHER beats a few times on the door. The YOUNG MAN tries unsuccessfully to open it. He backs off a few steps and stammers a few incomprehensible words. Again we hear the USHER's voice, now gentle and persuasive.) Are you there, young man?

YOUNG MAN: (voice thin, exhausted) Yes.

VOICE OF THE USHER: (gentle, persuasive) Open up, we'll talk. I already told you I adore the country, the glorious smell of the country when it rains . . . (furious) Open up, dammit! I can hear you whispering behind the door. I know you're there. Don't play with me! Idiot! I'll break your head open!

YOUNG MAN: But . . . I don't understand! What are you trying to do? It's locked from the outside!

VOICE OF THE USHER: (beating the door in a paroxysm of rage) You animal! Open up! Now! Open, open, open!

(Rashly the YOUNG MAN stretches his arm toward the door. Before his hand can grasp the latch, the door suddenly opens. The USHER enters, pushing a rolling table set with plates, platters, and a bottle in a cooling bucket. In spite of his screaming just before, he's humming and very content. He has shaved and rubbed his face so that the skin is smooth and polished, powdered, radiant. The YOUNG MAN watches him, stupefied.)

USHER: (smiling, as though it had all been a joke) But where's the young man's appetite? I had to beg you to open up. Perhaps you like being locked in?

YOUNG MAN: What are you saying? How was I going to open up?

USHER: I don't know, but I know it was locked. I had barely left last night when you locked it. I heard very clearly the sound of the key in the lock. I'm not deaf.

YOUNG MAN: That's a lie! You know very well the door was locked from the outside!

USHER: (drily) No, I don't know anything. You suspect that I played a trick on you, the point of which I can't even guess. I suspect you, so we're even. But I'm right!

YOUNG MAN: How was I going to open the door, you want to tell me? With what key?

USHER: (angry) What's it to me? I'm not some little boy who lets others slam the door in his face. The game's over, kid. I'll make sure you don't repeat this stupid joke. From now on, *I* will lock the door. (Suddenly, he starts humming. He busies himself preparing the plates. His manner is smiling and conscientious. He raises his head and looks toward the YOUNG MAN, who is unmoving and downcast. Cordially.) Oh sir, don't be like that! Dear sir, let's be friends! Anyone can get carried away for a moment, no reason to be bitter. Look at this. (Automatically, the YOUNG MAN touches his beard.) Yes, the young man has a tough beard, I saw it as soon as I came in. But don't worry. You still look terrific. Ooh, that smells delicious! We may have other imperfections, but as for attention to detail . . . silence! . . . as when you hear the national anthem! (He steps back a few steps and studies the way he has set the table. Laughs.) I laugh because . . . this should be somebody's last meal . . . Yes, it really should.

YOUNG MAN: (pale) Who? . . . Whose?

USHER: Somebody condemned to die. A meal for somebody at the end of his rope! (laughs) For the eve of the sad event, the end of the road. And it really looks like it! . . . Imagine how they must eat. With their stomachs in knots. May as well serve them stones! What a waste! (He laughs happily. After a moment, he sees the YOUNG MAN has collapsed on a chair. Affectionately.) What is it?

YOUNG MAN: You . . . you said that . . . that it's the last . . .

USHER: (smiling) No, no sir! Calm yourself. Do you think I would be capable of such tactlessness? It looks like it, but it's not. It's not, it's not! I assure you! (He laughs. Pours a drink and holds it out.) Don't be such a coward. Drink. (The YOUNG MAN drinks. Affectionately.) Better? If I'd thought you would react so, I'd have kept my thoughts to myself. What a sensitive soul you are! Permit me an observation?

YOUNG MAN: Yes.

USHER: Young man, one of your faults is that you worry too much. When you came in with the tall one and the small one, I saw right away that you worry too much. Others, no—they come gladly, primed for adventure. Of course, everyone's in the same pot.

YOUNG MAN: (visible reaction in his face) Everyone's in the same . . . ?

USHER: (laughs) See? You see? You're worrying again. It's an expression, and pretty common, at that. I'll tell you confidentially, your case is going well, better and better. I repeat, throw worry to the wind. Anything bad is temporary. It has to be. Life is brief. Do you know what I am?

YOUNG MAN: (timidly) An usher . . .

USHER: (brutally) Don't talk nonsense!

YOUNG MAN: No, no, I'm wrong.

USHER: (really enjoying it) I was a poor devil. And now, I'm no longer a poor devil.

YOUNG MAN: So what are you?

USHER: A little devil! (He laughs. Stops suddenly.) Come on, you're not laughing?

YOUNG MAN: (with a very pained smile) No . . . no.

USHER: (laughs) What are you afraid of?

YOUNG MAN: (trying to join in) Nothing. But why am I in the same . . . ?

USHER: (laughing) Because you are! Celebrate your own funeral! Do like me!

YOUNG MAN: (containing himself) You . . . you're celebrating . . . your funeral?

USHER: (quickly) No, yours! (laughs) They're going to cut off your head, so . . . laugh!

YOUNG MAN: (containing himself with effort, as though the USHER had told a hilarious joke) They're going to cut off my . . . That's . . . a good one! Very . . . funny! They're going to cut off my . . . No, I don't feel like it! . . . I don't want it! . . . (He gets up, involuntarily upsetting the chair.)

USHER: (laughs) I bet you they will! (The YOUNG MAN takes a few steps, holding back laughter, his fists clenched against his chest. Doubled over, he sits down on the bed. Laughing, the USHER approaches, gives him a hard, familiar clap on the back.) Something go down the wrong pipe?

(The YOUNG MAN gets up as though a spring has snapped inside him, arches back, and starts to laugh openly, grievedly.)

YOUNG MAN: Ay! Ay! Something go down the wrong pipe, you say? How funny! I never heard . . . anything . . . so . . . funny! . . . (laughs until he cries) Help me! He . . . elp me!

USHER: (who stopped guffawing as soon as the YOUNG MAN burst out laughing, watches him from the door. Shakes his head a little sadly, a little displeased.) That's no way to laugh, young man . . .

YOUNG MAN: (stops laughing from sheer exhaustion) I couldn't help it. It got to me. But how . . . idiotic.

USHER: Given your situation . . . I'm not saying this to worry you, but you're far from lucid. Quite far! Imagine if the Functionary happened to be coming down the hall, what would he think of me? Of you?

YOUNG MAN: But it isn't my fault! You started it!

USHER: (very irritated) I started it, what does that mean? Let's define our responsibilities. I don't want to censure you. There are tastes and there are tastes. But try not to harm us with your pleasures. Limit yourself to ruining your own reputation, not mine! (He leaves, slamming the door.)

YOUNG MAN: What are you saying? I made an effort and then . . . (Suddenly, he goes to the table and throws down two glasses of wine. He smiles, perks up. He eats while walking around the room. Methodically, he starts from the left-hand wall until he walks into the bed at the opposite end; then he turns around and starts again. He whispers a few unintelligible words. Suddenly, he stops dead, frightened. He looks incredulously at the walls. He retraces his path with visibly controlled steps.) No, it's impossible! What happened? What . . . ? What . . . ? (He rushes to the door and beats on it.) Usher! Usher!

USHER: (appearing immediately, amiably) You called, young man?

YOUNG MAN: (turning colors) The . . . the room!

USHER: (amiably) What's happening with the room?

YOUNG MAN: (terrified) It got smaller!

USHER: (takes the bottle and shows it to the YOUNG MAN. A friendly reproach.) Young man! I came running all the way from the street, and you called me for that!

YOUNG MAN: I'm not drunk!

USHER: (smiles) Well then?

YOUNG MAN: It's . . . smaller.

USHER: (smiles) You don't say!

YOUNG MAN: I was walking around the room counting my steps. It took ten steps to get from the wall to the bed, and now it takes eight! Eight . . .

USHER: (sits down on the bed, indulgent) Let's see. Do you always count your steps?

YOUNG MAN: Here. I walk and sing: (he sings in a thin voice) "Ten steps from the wall to the bed, ten steps from the bed to the wall, ten steps . . ." It's dumb, I know.

USHER: Have you always done this?

YOUNG MAN: Yes.

USHER: (full of wonder) You've spent your whole life counting your steps? How many have you counted, in total? Do you know? The figure must be astronomical.

YOUNG MAN: No. I meant to say . . . I started here, to distract myself, unconsciously.

USHER: Ah, unconsciously. I know this room. I can assure you that it hasn't changed a bit.

YOUNG MAN: (deflated) It hasn't?

USHER: No. (a pause) Wait . . . they did paint it once. They changed the color. Before, the walls were gray.

(The walls are gray.)

YOUNG MAN: Still, I counted ten steps, and now there are eight.

USHER: You're so stubborn! Or are you looking for a pretext to chat with me? (smiles, comes closer, ambiguous) How nice! A delicious surprise.

YOUNG MAN: (backs away) No. I'm sure.

USHER: So am I. It's easy to prove. (He walks from the bed to the wall. With decided inconsistency.) In effect, there are eight steps. There were *always* eight steps.

YOUNG MAN: It isn't possible!

USHER: Oh yes it is, sir. It's possible because what you say is completely unlikely. Have you always worried so about precision? What does your room at home measure?

YOUNG MAN: I don't know, exactly. I never paid attention.

USHER: (noncommittal) Curious, eh? Curious. (brief pause) Twelve feet?

YOUNG MAN: No. Less. It's a small room . . . nine by nine. That's it: nine by nine.

USHER: You're very wrong, sir! It measures twelve feet, five inches. Really strange that you don't know. I know, and I don't live there. How long have you?

YOUNG MAN: Two years.

USHER: And here, you check the room's measurements even before you get used to them. How do you know that the room isn't adapting to you?

YOUNG MAN: To me? In what way?

USHER: (aggressive) How should I know! Or do you think we're stealing it from you, bit by bit?

YOUNG MAN: No, I don't think that! It wasn't my intention to check anything. It happened in this room because I was idle. I was trying to entertain myself.

USHER: Since you were idle, you counted ten steps, then eight. Tomorrow you'll count twenty or fifty. Were your steps the same size? Are you sure?

YOUNG MAN: Yes.

USHER: No. You've been alone a long time. Too long. It isn't healthy—you start tripping over your own shadow.

YOUNG MAN: A long time? You'd just left!

USHER: (not listening) Solitude can make you hallucinate. You're not used to being alone.

YOUNG MAN: It wasn't because of that! The room . . .

USHER: Enough! Here's a comparison: in the dark you can see ghosts, but do ghosts exist? No, sir. The truth only emerges through comparison. Your eyes misjudged the size of the room. You called me in order to compare our truths. And I'm telling you, young man, you are absolutely wrong!

YOUNG MAN: Me? (looks around him, hesitates) It would be madness . . .

USHER: (pleased) Wouldn't it?

YOUNG MAN: Still, I would have bet . . .

USHER: Nothing, bet nothing and you can't lose!

YOUNG MAN: What?

USHER: (laughs calmingly) What do I know about what you could lose! Resign yourself. The Functionary will come to see you tomorrow, first thing. When the Functionary arrives early, he always brings good news. "Happiness can't wait," he says and gets up early. I advise you to be waiting for him, awake and tidy. He would never want you to go to any trouble, but I know he'd appreciate it.

YOUNG MAN: It won't be any trouble. Of course I'll be up and waiting for him. What time will he come?

USHER: Ten A.M. or ten P.M. Do you like the country, young man?

YOUNG MAN: Yes. I'd been to the country. It was precisely when I was getting off the train that they invited me to . . .

USHER: I know. I adore it. The sunsets! I'm a peasant at heart. I dream of buying a farm. I know how to castrate roosters . . . even hens! (He laughs. Then, seriously.) I love the healthy life, getting up with the sun, breathing fresh air, chewing the cud, gelding the stud . . . glorious!

(As the USHER speaks, the YOUNG MAN searches for the watch in his pocket. He doesn't find it. Then, very perplexed, he goes through his other pockets. A long, anguished scream is heard.)

YOUNG MAN: (jumps) Did you hear?

USHER: (stretches, yawning) What? No, no, I didn't hear.

Act 2

Scene 1

The same room, appreciably smaller. The curtains and the painting have disappeared. The YOUNG MAN, who lies sleeping, is illuminated from the side by a small light.

The USHER enters and turns on the center ceiling light. He is carrying a tin tray with a cup of coffee and a piece of bread. Rudely gruff, he puts the tray on the night table.

The YOUNG MAN wakes and sits up.

YOUNG MAN: Good morning. What time is it? I overslept.

USHER: (drily) Groundhog.

YOUNG MAN: The Functionary! Has the Functionary arrived?

USHER: (drily) Yes, he's arrived, but he's invisible.

YOUNG MAN: (laughs) Surely he won't be much longer. Right?

USHER: (drily) I can't answer any questions. None!

YOUNG MAN: You told me yourself he would come.

USHER: Yes. So what? He'll come, he won't come. That subject is not my concern. From now on, I will limit myself to my duties. It's the only way to come out ahead.

YOUNG MAN: Why do you say that? Have you had problems?

USHER: (furious) Plenty! So I'm asking you to eat your breakfast. I'm not here to stand around waiting for anyone!

YOUNG MAN: Right, of course. (He takes the cup and feels around for a spoon.)

USHER: There's sugar in it. I didn't bring the silverware today.

YOUNG MAN: It doesn't matter. (He takes a few sips of coffee in front of the USHER, who is manifestly impatient.) Leave the tray. Pick it up later.

USHER: (aggressive) No. I'll take it *now*. (with an ambiguous smile) Last night there was something missing.

YOUNG MAN: Missing?

USHER: Yes, I'm surprised at you. But of course one can only trust oneself. And not always.

YOUNG MAN: What are you insinuating?

USHER: I'm not insinuating. I'm making a statement. It's common among young men. A disgusting vice—going to cafés and stealing the sugar spoons.

YOUNG MAN: Stealing them?

USHER: Yes.

YOUNG MAN: But it must have fallen on the floor! How could you think I would pocket a sugar spoon?

USHER: It was silver, so why not?

YOUNG MAN: Because it's not my habit!

USHER: Your habits are your business. I only know what I can prove: I brought four pieces of silverware; I took back three. You're not the only one. Taking advantage of impunity. (furious) You all know you won't be tried for it! So you're calm! So you steal!

YOUNG MAN: You're slandering me! Damn whoever swiped the spoon! Why would I want it?

USHER: Thief!

YOUNG MAN: Quiet, I won't let you insult me!

USHER: Oh yes you will, as much as I like! Who knows what you've already taken.

YOUNG MAN: I repeat . . . I'll complain to the Functionary. I'll tell him about your stupid accusations!

USHER: Do it! I admire your cold-bloodedness. But it was my fault for being so naive. It was a mistake to trust you—with the silver, my confidences about the country, and all the rest. You'll pay for this, and dearly! You'll see!

(Silently, during the USHER's last words, the FUNCTIONARY appears in the doorway. He keeps his theatrical, invariably sympathetic, smiling manner.)

FUNCTIONARY: What were you saying? Don't get so upset. You'll get a headache. Calm down. The young man won't pay for anything. On the contrary! He's our guest, don't forget it. (Smiling, he approaches the YOUNG MAN.) How are you, my dear man? I'm happy to see you after so long! How I've missed our conversations! What a shame we've never been able to chat!

YOUNG MAN: (pale with indignation, extends his hand. Stammers.) Fine. He's accusing me . . . !

FUNCTIONARY: Of nothing! Trifles! I don't want to know. Silence! (to the USHER, with paternal severity) Get along, get along, son, back to work. No more delaying. You've got a lot to do this morning. (The USHER gathers the tray and, as he passes in front of the FUNCTIONARY, bows with exaggerated servile reverence, at the same time winking at him. The YOUNG MAN notes the familiar gesture of complicity, stupefied. The FUNCTIONARY, very pleased, rubs his hands.) Good, good, good! As they say in the theater, alone at last! (He laughs.)

YOUNG MAN: Sir, you really don't want to know . . .

FUNCTIONARY: Nothing, nothing, nothing. See, I tri-peat myself! (laughs, very pleased with his joke) Your case doesn't interest you? What apathy!

YOUNG MAN: It's that I'm . . . surprised, nauseated. To accuse me . . . !

FUNCTIONARY: (categorically) Not another word. Not another word about that! I abhor gossip. (softening) Do you want to talk about the weather, about art? I love opera.

YOUNG MAN: (miserable) Whatever you like.

FUNCTIONARY: No, you tell me.

YOUNG MAN: Do you have any news for me? The Usher told me that today, surely . . .

FUNCTIONARY: Sssshhh! Don't even mention him! He's a plague. (a pause) News I have, and very good, too! Excellent! But, why such a rush? *Vita longa, res breve.* (laughs)

YOUNG MAN: (laughs anxiously, awkwardly) So you do have news?

FUNCTIONARY: Such impatience! You plague me with questions! Let me breathe! I'm not as young as you are. How old are you?

YOUNG MAN: Twenty-two.

FUNCTIONARY: I noticed right away, twenty to forty, not one year more. I noticed because of your impatience, young man, your temperament! (laughs) Otherwise, you'd act like me! You would perform in a measured way, with voluptuous slowness. I scarcely lift my arm for fear of disturbing the flow of time. (sits) Ah, youth! My father went to prostitutes. He told me so himself. What an old goat! Me, no. Moderation, continence, impotence. (laughs) You're so serious and quiet! Don't you ever laugh?

YOUNG MAN: Yes, of course.

FUNCTIONARY: I knew you weren't going to lie to me! What were you and the Usher laughing so hard about, the other morning?

YOUNG MAN: The other morning?

FUNCTIONARY: Yes. I happened to be walking down the hall. I asked the Usher. He said, "The boy told a joke. He's very happy, a cheerful character." I approve. The young should enjoy themselves.

YOUNG MAN: I told a joke?

FUNCTIONARY: Yes, that's why it surprises me to see you so serious. Tell me the joke, I like to laugh. At good, clean humor, naturally.

YOUNG MAN: There was no joke. It was . . .

FUNCTIONARY: (very interested and smiling) Yes . . .

YOUNG MAN: Nothing, imagine that . . . I don't know how to explain . . .

FUNCTIONARY: (interested and smiling) A dirty joke?

YOUNG MAN: No.

FUNCTIONARY: (laughs) So you've been amusing the Usher with dirty jokes? I won't protest, even though he was working and shouldn't have. Tell it to me.

YOUNG MAN: No. It wasn't like that.

FUNCTIONARY: (claps him familiarly on the back) Come on! I don't usually, but just this once . . . I'll tell you one. I know thousands.

YOUNG MAN: I repeat, it wasn't like that. I really don't know why the Usher started to laugh, or at least, I don't remember. I didn't feel like laughing . . .

FUNCTIONARY: (dry and distrusting) How strange! . . . Were you laughing at me, perhaps?

YOUNG MAN: No, please! How could you think so?

FUNCTIONARY: Well, what was he laughing at? You're in no situation to laugh.

YOUNG MAN: (livid) I'm in no situation?

FUNCTIONARY: (smiles instantly) Because your situation is neither grave nor comical: *entièrement normal*. How's my French, monsieur? I studied with Madame Ninon de Lenclos.[2] (looks at the YOUNG MAN, who obviously doesn't know Ninon de Lenclos)

YOUNG MAN: It seems excellent. You speak very well.

FUNCTIONARY: (testing) *Bon jour, bon jour!* (alarmed) Or *bon soir?* (He takes the YOUNG MAN's watch from his pocket and looks at it in front of him, naturally, so as not to be accused by the evidence.) Didn't I say so? I'm behind! My damn habit of stopping to talk with idiots, I get enthused, go astray. Young man, most esteemed young man, there's good news. What you've been hoping for, perhaps. To never deceive is my greatest happiness. Are you listening?

YOUNG MAN: Yes.

FUNCTIONARY: We have a surprise. (falls silent)

YOUNG MAN: I'm listening, sir.

FUNCTIONARY: You can't imagine what it might be?

YOUNG MAN: (imagining something awful) Yes, yes, I can imagine.

FUNCTIONARY: Your brief stay with us, *avec nous,* must be unforgettable for you. We have brought . . . Guess!

YOUNG MAN: What?

FUNCTIONARY: Yes, we went looking for her in your own room. (roguish) Who is it?

YOUNG MAN: (dumbfounded) What? I have nobody.

FUNCTIONARY: (satisfied) Think.

YOUNG MAN: Nobody. (tries to smile) At least, not in my room. Is this . . . the news?

FUNCTIONARY: What were you expecting? Aren't you pleased?

YOUNG MAN: No. I believed . . . believed I was going free!

FUNCTIONARY: No one's stopping you from believing it. (touches a buzzer on the wall, at the same time calling) Usher, Usher! (to the YOUNG MAN) Did you know there was a buzzer here?

YOUNG MAN: No. Then I won't be leaving today.

FUNCTIONARY: Why are you so sure? What's certain in this world? Don't touch.

YOUNG MAN: Do I get out of here today?

FUNCTIONARY: (categorically) No. Let's press the buzzer, maybe it'll work. *Nessuna cosa e certa.*

YOUNG MAN: Then when? I don't wish to bother you, Mr. Functionary, but they're strict at the office. What excuse will I give for my absence? I'm afraid of losing my job. I don't have any other income, and my rent is running since I'm still occupying my room, in a manner of speaking.

FUNCTIONARY: Your rent is running? (laughs) Nice image! (smiling) We'll try not to let that happen, let you occupy two rooms at once. What with the housing shortage!

YOUNG MAN: Then I can count . . . ?

FUNCTIONARY: (calmingly) On everything! Believe me, I can see that, in spite of your situation, you're thinking of the office.

YOUNG MAN: (worried) In spite of?

FUNCTIONARY: Your excellent situation! Others would think of lost sheep. Not you. You're a young man with a future. (extremely bored) What a bore! Did you hear the buzzer?

YOUNG MAN: No.

FUNCTIONARY: But it was working. Not that I have any doubts, but it's better to make sure. (shouts, while pushing the buzzer) Usher, Usher!

VOICE OF THE USHER: Coming, sir!

(The USHER appears, happily holding a porcelain doll in his arms. It is an enormous doll, dressed with an excessive profusion of lace and tulle, completely vulgar and unchildlike, with ringlets and a little mouth, puckered and red.)

FUNCTIONARY: (pleased) Ah, how opportune! You read my mind. (He takes the doll and, very proudly, presents it to the YOUNG MAN.) Recognize her?

YOUNG MAN: (aghast) That vile thing! I was expecting . . . I can't understand why you would bring me this. What for?

FUNCTIONARY: Oh no, sir! You should thank me!

YOUNG MAN: Excuse me. It doesn't even belong to me! It belongs to my landlady.

FUNCTIONARY: But you had her in your room! Where was she, Usher?

USHER: In the young man's room.

FUNCTIONARY: (boastfully) I already know that!

USHER: She was on the bed, like this. (takes the doll and puts it on the bed in a compromising position) In the young man's bed, that's right. (laughs) Did you sleep with her, young man? Not a very good substitute.

FUNCTIONARY: (furious) Have you no shame, Usher! Restrain yourself!

USHER: Sorry.

YOUNG MAN: (timidly) I was expecting a few shirts, a change of clothes. Of course if tomorrow I can go . . .

FUNCTIONARY: (smiling) You could as easily come . . . (laughs) We brought you art, young man. What do shirts matter? You can wear a dirty shirt for another day, for another week, for a thousand years. But without art, young man . . . we would asphyxiate. Thank us.

USHER: The landlady begged me to take care of her. "I'm only letting you take her to the young man because he's a sensitive soul," she said. She expresses herself very well for a woman who runs a rooming house.

YOUNG MAN: I hate that doll. I didn't know how to get rid of it without offending the landlady. Too big. It's a nuisance in the room, an aberration.

USHER: (amused) An aberration, perhaps . . . you did have her on your bed.

YOUNG MAN: So what?

USHER: So they're all the same in the dark, right? (laughs)

FUNCTIONARY: (paternally) Usher, watch your language. I've told you. It's your only fault.

YOUNG MAN: The tenants pass it around. No one wants it. No one dares smash it. They're afraid of the landlady. Me too.

USHER: (takes the doll, examines it) Not a mark on her. Perfect condition.

FUNCTIONARY: (amused) No, they're not afraid of the landlady. It has to do with art, young man. Don't you understand? That's why not one of you has smashed her. Art is all that deserves to last—lofty sentiments, things and beings coming to life. You haven't smashed the doll so as to assure that there will be beauty in the world, order. In a word: so the trees can keep growing and putting forth new leaves, so the earth does not become a desolate wasteland. (takes a breath) Ah!

USHER: (proud) Very good, sir! You were eloquent!

FUNCTIONARY: (modest) Thank you.

YOUNG MAN: (letting out a timid little laugh) She's so ugly!

FUNCTIONARY: Yes, I accept that. She's an unpleasing vehicle, but she accomplishes her aims.

YOUNG MAN: Her aims?

FUNCTIONARY: Yes, young man, her aims. I'm glad you're always asking questions. It serves art well.

YOUNG MAN: I wouldn't want to contradict you, sir, but I would love to smash her. As soon as I can, I hide her under the bed. And even so, I have nightmares.

FUNCTIONARY: You're fooling yourself, young man. You're protecting the doll. So are the other tenants. That's why she's intact. Smash her.

YOUNG MAN: Smash her!

FUNCTIONARY: Don't repeat. It sounds like an echo. Tear her limb from limb.

YOUNG MAN: (after a silence) But she isn't mine!

FUNCTIONARY: What do you care! Who's stopping you?

YOUNG MAN: What for? I don't understand what for.

FUNCTIONARY: Didn't you want to?

YOUNG MAN: Not like this.

FUNCTIONARY: Then how?

YOUNG MAN: By accident!

FUNCTIONARY: Accidents don't just happen. Stumble over this chair, and good-bye doll!

USHER: (hands the doll to the YOUNG MAN. Smiles.) Go ahead, young man!

YOUNG MAN: (looking for a way out) I think . . . Mr. Functionary, you were right, I don't understand anything. Why pressure me? How does that serve art?

FUNCTIONARY: (furious) You damn hypocrite! Smash her!

YOUNG MAN: (frightened) If you order me, I'll do it.

FUNCTIONARY: No way. What do I care? I'm leaving.

YOUNG MAN: No, no! I'll do it!

USHER: Go ahead, young man! Here's the chair. (He puts the chair in front of the YOUNG MAN.)

YOUNG MAN: (after a silence) I can't.

FUNCTIONARY: (irritated) But, tell me, weren't you dying to smash her? Take your pleasure.

YOUNG MAN: I can't. My landlady. We couldn't even upset a glass at the table. She'd bitch all day. I don't want to hear it.

FUNCTIONARY: (with brutal candor) And why would you hear it? When?

YOUNG MAN: (stupidly) When . . . ?

FUNCTIONARY: (furious) Put wax in your ears! Get this piece of shit out of my sight! Smash her!

YOUNG MAN: (tries to obey, but courage fails him. Anguished.) But why? It doesn't seem right to me. You yourself said she represented art.

FUNCTIONARY: And I'm saying now she's garbage!

YOUNG MAN: (as though the doll were burning hot, puts it on the bed) She isn't mine! She belongs to my landlady. Forgive me, but I can't smash it. (anguished) Am I never going to get out of here?

(A silence. Then, as though the question amused him, the FUNCTIONARY drops his anger, laughs good-naturedly. The USHER immediately echoes him.)

FUNCTIONARY: How could you think something so outrageous?

YOUNG MAN: (looks at him in suspense, then also smiles with relief) I was scared. Impunity to this extreme, Mr. Functionary! If it weren't for my landlady's screaming, I'd smash it with pleasure. It's a vile thing, I know.

FUNCTIONARY: (drily) I wouldn't be so sure.

YOUNG MAN: (surprised) You don't think it's vile?

FUNCTIONARY: I couldn't possibly speak to so delicate a question, without giving it some thought. I'll meditate on it tonight. What time is it, young man? (hurriedly) No, no. Don't tell me the hour, I know the hour. Every hour, till the sun falls from the sky. And after all, who keeps track of time? Not me. So time forgets I exist. (laughs) What an afternoon! Till tomorrow. (warmly extends his hand) I'll come tomorrow. Sit and wait for me. We'll chat. Optimism. *Bonne nuit. Buona notte!*

(He leaves. With a surprised and stupid expression, the YOUNG MAN watches him move away. Then he looks at the doll and places it carefully on the floor, under the bed.)

USHER: (moves closer, sweetly) Do you want me to go to your house? If you give me the key to your room, I can bring your shaving things, a change of clothes.

YOUNG MAN: What for?

USHER: You look like shit. With all due respect, sir.

YOUNG MAN: So, I'm never getting out of here?

USHER: You get everything backward. Probably tomorrow.

YOUNG MAN: The Functionary didn't assure me of it.

USHER: He's afraid. Haven't you noticed how he always laughs when he's afraid? He promised you he'd come tomorrow and bring good news. Otherwise, he'll disappear. He promises to come and disappears. (laughs)

YOUNG MAN: (fearful) He won't do that to me, will he? He'll come, won't he?

USHER: (irritated) Enough already! (friendly) Are you pleased with us?

YOUNG MAN: (not knowing what to say) Yes. (after a pause) Yes, yes!

USHER: We never get tired of talking about you. We remark on your gestures, your generosity, even your little tics.

YOUNG MAN: (worried) My tics?

USHER: Yes, those too. Few lodgers have been able to count on so much sympathy. They can't count on any, in fact. The Functionary is enchanted. I won't talk about myself. We have so much in common!

YOUNG MAN: Who?

USHER: Us! The country! (very cloying) Once again! (smiles) You came here from the country, and I dream of going from here to the country. Let me smell you. (He smells him.) Daisies, clover. The smell of the henhouse, too.

YOUNG MAN: (offended) Not the henhouse! I didn't get close to any hen.

USHER: Pity. But someday you'll get close, and the smell will stay with you. A lovely smell, like lavender. I'll keep you abreast of your situation.

YOUNG MAN: Do you know anything?

USHER: It can't be improved.

YOUNG MAN: Have they verified my name yet?

USHER: They're working on it. Henfo.

YOUNG MAN: No, my name's not Henfo!

USHER: They're working on it; they verified your name's not Henfo. But finally, it doesn't matter what they verify. You'll soon be free. It's imminent.

YOUNG MAN: You're lying!

USHER: I thank you for your trust!

YOUNG MAN: Why didn't the Functionary tell me?

USHER: Weakness.

YOUNG MAN: I don't get it.

USHER: You don't have to.

YOUNG MAN: I . . . I don't believe it!

USHER: Word of honor! Why would I lie?

YOUNG MAN: You're really not joking?

USHER: (with an exaggerated gesture) Me?

YOUNG MAN: It would be stupid, cruel . . . You know what it means to me.

USHER: (indifferent) And to me.

YOUNG MAN: Then I'm begging you, tell me the truth.

USHER: Death be my witness. You will go free within . . . hours, tomorrow first thing. But why am I telling you? What's in it for me?

YOUNG MAN: You've taken a weight off. (laughs) I was a little worried. Why? Just nervous, I guess.

USHER: (very understanding) Don't blame yourself. Blame human nature, young man.

YOUNG MAN: Right.

USHER: (interrupts him) Don't thank me! Know where I'm going tomorrow?

YOUNG MAN: No.

USHER: To the country! And here is where I'll see your heartfelt gratitude.

YOUNG MAN: I don't understand, but if there's any way I can be of use to you . . .

USHER: You will be of use. See, I have to check the time very frequently. I've got to wake up by seven so I can get the train at seven-thirty. I noticed that you have a beautiful watch. Family memento?

YOUNG MAN: Yes, a gift from my father.

USHER: Would you be so kind as to let me have it for a few years?

YOUNG MAN: (a pause. Discouraged.) I don't have it.

USHER: What did you say?

YOUNG MAN: I lost it.

USHER: (incredulous) You lost it *here?*

YOUNG MAN: I suppose in the room.

USHER: (takes a step backward) My good man, if you don't wish to lend your damn watch, say so and not a word more about it. But no subterfuge. I know very well that you couldn't have lost your watch in this room.

YOUNG MAN: Well, I'm telling you again that I don't have it!

USHER: Well, I'm telling you you're lying!

YOUNG MAN: Look. I put it under the pillow. (lifts the pillow) It's not there. I don't have it on me. It disappeared.

USHER: Whom are you trying to hoodwink?

YOUNG MAN: No one! I'm telling you it disappeared! Are you deaf? What am I going to tell my father? I won't tell him anything: he's dead. But it's just the same, as if I had to see him and give him an accounting. My God, what excuse am I going to give my own conscience for having so stupidly lost it?

USHER: Isn't this the same bullshit you pulled with the sugar spoon? Seems to me you don't like lending your things. Stingy bastard!

YOUNG MAN: Go to hell!

USHER: (pushes him down on the floor) Better be careful, little man. Or have you swallowed the story that you're leaving to-morrow? (goes through his pockets, turns the bedclothes up-side down) You don't have it! You did this on purpose! Idiot! You got yourself robbed!

YOUNG MAN: (getting to his feet) I got . . .

USHER: (at once furious and disconsolate) Don't repeat! Idiot! You are an idiot! You can't deny it. Just my luck! Go through all this for nothing. Why is he so damned insatiable! What does he want all these watches for? Well, I won't be left with nothing!

YOUNG MAN: Who is "he"? What are you saying?

USHER: (hurls himself at the YOUNG MAN) You don't know? Idiot! Idiot! I could kill you for being such an idiot!

(blackout)

Scene 2

The set is dark. The area will appear noticeably smaller relative to the previous scene. The only pieces of furniture are a cot and a chair, which take up practically the whole space. We hear the coughing and breathing of someone who has a bad cold.

VOICE OF THE FUNCTIONARY: Can I turn on the light?

VOICE OF THE YOUNG MAN: Yes, why not. I'm awake. Go ahead.

FUNCTIONARY: (turns on the light, snuffling) Sorry to bother you at this hour, but it's my only free moment. I said to myself: better early than never.

YOUNG MAN: (sitting on the cot, with his clothes rumpled. He has a black eye. Moves as though he'd been beaten up.) Please, how could you be bothering me. On the contrary. I'm very grateful that you've come. I see you have a bad cold.

FUNCTIONARY: No kidding! I caught a chill coming out of the theater. The warm air inside, the cold night—to make a long story short, today I'm dead. It's a miracle I'm on my feet, (beats his chest) pure spirit. Do you like the theater? I went to hear *Lucia di Lammermoor*. The mad scene made my hair stand on end, lifted me right out of my seat. I love bel canto, young man, the opera. I myself, ahem . . . ! (He's hoarse and smiles timidly, his eyes downcast.)

YOUNG MAN: (doesn't understand) You yourself?

FUNCTIONARY: Isn't it amazing?

YOUNG MAN: (still doesn't understand) Ah . . . ! How nice! You yourself!

FUNCTIONARY: You don't believe me? Happens all the time. People don't consider one's sensibility. Everyone sees the Functionary. The times we live in! Listen.

(He puts his hand on his chest, takes a step forward, stumbles over the cot, leans against it, and sings a few notes with a very loud, rough voice.)

YOUNG MAN: (finally getting it) Ah, what a beautiful voice! Of course! But how was I to know? My congratulations.

FUNCTIONARY: Wait! (sings again and then looks at the YOUNG MAN. Waits for his reaction.)

YOUNG MAN: (stupidly and sincerely impressed) How extraordinary! If I had that voice! . . . You've got a real artistic gift. Are you singing anyplace?

FUNCTIONARY: (flushed with pleasure) Singing anyplace? Not even in my dreams! With this cold! If I could drop the job! . . . But at this stage of life, who can risk it? Not me. I'd sing at La Scala. (suddenly) Ah, your case, young man! We lose so much time talking! But what happened to your eye?

YOUNG MAN: I had a . . . I had an incident with the Usher.

FUNCTIONARY: What kind of incident? He hit you, maybe?

YOUNG MAN: Yes, he hit me.

FUNCTIONARY: (drily) Ah, so you're in the habit of accusing those who aren't present?

YOUNG MAN: Accusing?

FUNCTIONARY: Then what are you doing?

YOUNG MAN: I didn't mean to, honest. I only wanted to explain to you what happened.

FUNCTIONARY: Be brief, don't use up my time. I don't like whispering behind people's backs.

YOUNG MAN: I'm not! How could you think . . . ?

FUNCTIONARY: (interrupting) For me there aren't subordinates and then all the others. There are friends and enemies. So, expound your grievances with precision, and we'll be done with it. Solomonic judgment, my dear man.

YOUNG MAN: It . . . it was a mistake . . .

FUNCTIONARY: (harshly) Quiet! Judge not, if you don't want to be judged! (a pause, impatient) Well? What are you waiting for?

YOUNG MAN: The Usher asked to borrow my watch.

FUNCTIONARY: How brazen! For that you hit him?

YOUNG MAN: No, he hit me.

FUNCTIONARY: I'd understood the opposite.

YOUNG MAN: No, look at my eye.

FUNCTIONARY: It's black. Well, why did you hit the Usher?

YOUNG MAN: No, sir. I didn't hit him. He came . . .

FUNCTIONARY: Don't say "he," say "the Usher." Better to avoid all familiarity.

YOUNG MAN: The Usher came and . . .

FUNCTIONARY: (abstracted) You could say "the honorable Usher . . ." *C'est plus joli.*

YOUNG MAN: The honorable Usher came and asked to borrow my watch.

FUNCTIONARY: How brazen! For that you hit him?

YOUNG MAN: (confused) No, no sir, he hit me.

FUNCTIONARY: Nevertheless, the facts are very clear. The facts sing, the song is proof. The Usher came, he asked to borrow your watch, you got furious and hit him. Well, let's see, whose watch was it?

YOUNG MAN: Mine. A memento of my father.

FUNCTIONARY: Fine, but the Usher is old enough to be your father. I don't understand why you acted with such rage.

YOUNG MAN: I assure you, I didn't even raise my hand. I wouldn't have had the nerve.

FUNCTIONARY: Why not? Didn't he deserve it?

YOUNG MAN: Sir, it seems to me there's a misunderstanding. (touching his eye) It . . . it hurts.

FUNCTIONARY: The Usher has no mark on his eye, but I can't make a judgment on that basis. You must realize. Let me see, haven't you had this from birth?

YOUNG MAN: No, sir. I didn't have it yesterday.

FUNCTIONARY: Accidents like this do happen. You go to bed without a toothache, but you wake up with a toothache. That's how it must have happened with you. Perhaps you think that I've had this cold from birth? And you weren't even up and waiting when I arrived. What lack of courtesy! I'm good, but not stupid.

YOUNG MAN: I'm sorry. I didn't feel well. I'm worn out.

FUNCTIONARY: Is that my fault? I don't feel well either, but here I am, doing my duty. Let's dispense with the personal, young man, because if we keep on with this "I feel, I don't feel," we'll never finish. You know that I have only a few minutes, and you're delaying me. Are you doing it on purpose?

YOUNG MAN: No! No, sir. I can't find the words to tell you how I regret this.

FUNCTIONARY: Ah, finally I hear a careful sentence! Do you want to know what's happening with your case, *l'affaire?*

YOUNG MAN: Yes, please.

FUNCTIONARY: (pleased and pompous) *Laissez-faire!*

YOUNG MAN: I . . . I don't understand.

FUNCTIONARY: (conceited) Why don't you study? The future belongs to those who study languages. I gave you an interesting message, and with what result? None! You got up on the wrong side of the bed this morning.

YOUNG MAN: (at the end of his strength) Yes. Would you be so kind as to . . .

FUNCTIONARY: Repeat it! As though it cost nothing! Let's make an effort. Your case is going well, wellissimo. Do you want more details? I'll give you some. You have a most unusual name! How do you pronounce it? Hencau, Henco, Hempo? Oh, but it doesn't matter! For the final results it doesn't matter a bit. I wish to congratulate you, now. (laughs) Lucky young man! Tomorrow, at this hour, you . . . (He lets out a happy laugh, cut off by snorting and coughing. He takes out a handkerchief and blows his nose. The YOUNG MAN smiles but, overcome with emotion, sits down on the bed and hides his face in his hands. The FUNCTIONARY lets his own face appear behind the hankie and watches the YOUNG MAN, charmed and amused. Then he draws close and leans toward him. In a confidential, almost tender, tone.) Come on, what's this, what's this? It didn't go so badly between us, did it? Life is a dream. So is death. Don't be frightened. Only it may cost you a little to dream . . .

YOUNG MAN: (lifts his head. He hasn't understood or hasn't been listening.) What are you saying?

FUNCTIONARY: (moves off toward the door, smiling happily) If only I were young! You don't know how I envy you. Ah, youth! I would devote myself to singing! (sings) La, la, la! Till tomorrow, son, till tomorrow. Although tomorrow we won't be seeing each other anymore! Who knows!

(He exits. The YOUNG MAN rubs his face, tries to walk around the shrunken room, stumbles over the cot. He lifts the doll from the floor, looks at it, and ends by placing it on the cot, awkwardly arranging it, then sitting next to it as though he were watching over someone. After a moment, the USHER appears with a washbasin and a compress.)

USHER: (offhand) Do you want to put on this compress? It'll help. The Functionary always advises me to act with restraint. "Hit, but try not to hurt anyone," he says. Even though this time he didn't scold me. He's so understanding! Here. (He puts the compress on the YOUNG MAN's eye.) Hold it. Does it hurt?

YOUNG MAN: (pushes him away. Holds the compress.) No. Not now.

USHER: (proud of himself) I didn't go to the country today. Do you remember? I dreamed of breathing clover and daisies.

"Go on, Usher," the Functionary implored me, "you need a little sunshine, a little relaxation. Amusement." But I couldn't leave! In my own flesh I felt every punch I gave you. I shook with remorse.

YOUNG MAN: (with great effort) I don't want . . . to know anything about you.

USHER: You've got to understand me! My great yearning to return to the country, to a healthy, bucolic life, often drives me to actions not exactly in good taste, even a little contemptible, I admit. But is it my fault?

YOUNG MAN: You know. I don't know.

USHER: "I don't know." Your attitude is very convenient! (He grabs the compress.) I commit contemptible acts under the influence of lyrical needs. Don't I deserve some tolerance? Like with the watch, for instance. Couldn't the gentleman excuse me? That was a misunderstanding! Young man, perhaps all of life is a misunderstanding. Do we lead the same life? Well then, why the same end? Is it just? How can you help but lose patience?

YOUNG MAN: I'm not interested. I'm getting out of here tomorrow. We won't be seeing each other anymore. And I'll tell you now—I'm glad!

USHER: Oh no! You can't disappear leaving me with the remorse. I can't stand it! Pardon my attitude with the watch. I acted with too much vehemence. After all, the Functionary was within his rights.

YOUNG MAN: (at once astonished and terrified) Do you think he took my watch?

USHER: (natural) Yes, he usually does. Then he sells them.

YOUNG MAN: You're lying to me! The Functionary is a gentleman! He's . . . a father . . . yes, a father.

USHER: Who doubts it! I wouldn't permit half a word against the Functionary.

YOUNG MAN: But you're telling me that he stole my watch!

USHER: That he took it! Careful with your language, young man.

YOUNG MAN: It's the same thing!

USHER: No. I maintained that he took your watch. Between that and stealing it there's quite a distance, wouldn't you say?

YOUNG MAN: (stammers) My . . . *my* watch!

USHER: (very understanding) From your father, wasn't it? It hurts to lose family mementos. It isn't the intrinsic value that you regret. It's the smile with which the watch was handed down, the words . . .

YOUNG MAN: (low) How do you know?

USHER: (with a little laugh) I intuit.

YOUNG MAN: Then please, answer this, only this: Did the Functionary take my watch?

USHER: In the first place, what do you want me to answer?

YOUNG MAN: Yes or no.

USHER: (laughs) I suppose . . .

YOUNG MAN: (upset) Impossible! He assured me—no, no, he didn't assure me . . . out of . . . excessive honesty, in case some unforeseen event should prove him wrong—that I was leaving tomorrow. And now you say . . . Why, why would he take my watch? He should have asked me for it! (nearly screaming) He's a Functionary, not just anybody!

USHER: Who says otherwise? I think you want to believe that the Functionary did not take your watch. Think what you like.

YOUNG MAN: It is not what I want to think! I refuse to believe such infamy! "I'll be like a father to you," he told me.

USHER: He is! One father gives you a watch, the other takes it away. (laughs) I was joking. You could have lost the watch in the room. Did you check the room? Did you check your pockets? Speaking of pockets, do you have any money?

YOUNG MAN: What for?

USHER: What do you mean, what for? Don't you want to be informed of news that closely affects you?

YOUNG MAN: What news? I'm getting out of here tomorrow. That's what I have to worry about.

USHER: You'd do well to worry. Anyone can see that.

YOUNG MAN: What?

USHER: Oh, no! I hate to be pressured.

YOUNG MAN: What do you know?

USHER: Gratitude is a worthy sentiment, but you can't buy anything with it, not even a hen. So how do I reconcile my appetite for hens with . . . ?

YOUNG MAN: (nervously takes out his wallet and hands over a few bills) Enough! What's happening? Have they pushed up the date? Am I getting out today? Is that it?

USHER: (laughs and waves the bills in front of his face) I won't say anything now! I won't say a thing! What wretchedness! Keep your filthy money! (But he pockets it.) Damned skinflint! You're about to . . . I shut my mouth. Good night!

YOUNG MAN: Come back! How can you leave me like this?

USHER: You won't get a word out of me! Wretch! (He exits. Impotently wringing his hands, the YOUNG MAN walks around, banging into the furniture. Suddenly, he heads toward the door and calls out. The USHER, who apparently expected this, appears immediately. Very pleased.) Sir?

YOUNG MAN: Would the wallet help? (He holds it out. Meekly.) Please, won't you talk to me? The Functionary promised that tomorrow . . .

USHER: (without listening to him, takes the wallet and examines it) A little worn around the edges, young man. (He keeps it.) Can't you offer me something else? The price went up.

YOUNG MAN: But . . . ! You're a . . . !

USHER: Let's not argue! If you don't agree, I'm going. Immediately, *mutis eterno.* In the end, it's your fault for going out with so little money.

YOUNG MAN: What do you want me to give you? The impossible? Don't you see that I have nothing with me? When I get out . . .

USHER: (cutting him off) Let's not count on it!

YOUNG MAN: Am I never getting out of here?

USHER: I didn't say that. Your future doesn't interest me. I don't get involved in anybody's future. It's as though you were dead. (hastens to add) In a manner of speaking.

YOUNG MAN: Do you want the doll?

USHER: That piece of junk? No! Anyway, how are you going to give me something that isn't yours?

YOUNG MAN: Forgive me. But what can I offer you? I have nothing! Don't you understand?

USHER: I'm leaving!

YOUNG MAN: (subdues him, humbly) Please . . . I didn't mean to offend you. I lose my head. What do you know? Surely you understand my concern.

USHER: I do understand it, I share it. The price hasn't risen for any spurious reason, young man. Old news costs the most. Yes sir, already half an hour ago, there I was, my ear to the door, learning, by chance, what fate holds for you next. Perhaps you don't know what half an hour means in the life of a piece of news? It can mean a lot. It can happen that it goes unknown, is transformed into a secret. And the secret is like death. (smiles) I don't mean to upset you. No one knows what the secret holds. Maybe . . . yes . . . death.

YOUNG MAN: (lucid) My death!

USHER: Enough with your death! I'm talking in general. We could turn to the particular, if you wish. Search your person. Maybe you've forgotten something valuable in one of your pockets.

YOUNG MAN: (checking his pockets, takes out a key ring) I have this key ring. Maybe that could serve.

USHER: (examines it. Impertinent.) Without keys?

YOUNG MAN: They disappeared.

USHER: Oh, right, when we took everything from your room.

YOUNG MAN: From my room?

USHER: No, from my room. (keeps the key ring)

YOUNG MAN: You said yourself you took everything from my room.

USHER: What circumspection. You could exhaust the patience of a saint. Didn't we bring you the doll? What did you think? That we climbed in the window? We won't discuss it, because I've zipped up my mouth and the subject is closed.

YOUNG MAN: (his voice weak) Won't you talk?

USHER: (friendly) Naturally! I could have given you the news anyway. What's it to me? There needn't have been such a scandal. Why scream? (a silence) Are you comfortable there?

YOUNG MAN: Yes.

USHER: That's how I like you—happy! Don't you want to sit down? No? It would be better. If you sit down, your knees won't give out. In any case, the floor is closer. (He laughs. The YOUNG MAN sits down.) Very good! Consider this a parting gift. In effect, it is a gift to tell you such surprising news for so little. (The YOUNG MAN, eaten through with impatience, is starting to get up.) No, sit down! Are you ready?

YOUNG MAN: (at the end of his strength) Yes.

USHER: The news is the following: At midnight, the walls will fall in on you. (happily) The same as if you hadn't known. Without exception, the news is death. Death is like a secret, it makes you see what you don't know.

YOUNG MAN: (can't find his voice, trembles, finally leaps up) You bastard, what are you saying?

USHER: A little moderation, please. I would have liked to give you other news, your upcoming marriage, for example. Unfortunately, no women. I'm no misogynist, but in the news there weren't any women.

YOUNG MAN: Listen to me. You're not serious, are you?

USHER: Do you remember the screams?

YOUNG MAN: Yes.

USHER: You see!

YOUNG MAN: You're wrong, you're totally wrong. Their screaming is a vice. There's nothing to worry about. The Functionary explained it to me.

USHER: (worldly) Very interesting. What did he explain?

YOUNG MAN: Just that—their screaming is a vice. Time makes them scream, it passes without touching them, as if they were dead. So they scream to call time, to make it respond and touch them, make them grow old, make them . . . return to the office. (The USHER laughs. The YOUNG MAN is obstinate.) That happens to the others. I myself . . . At times, I want to scream. I get anxious, when I think of the office.

USHER: They don't all work in offices.

YOUNG MAN: They scream because they're tired, they're bored, but not because they're dying!

USHER: (with suspicious acquiescence) No, no, they're not dying.

YOUNG MAN: You were lying to me.

USHER: They kill them. You should recognize, it's not like lying in bed after a long life letting death come, like a dream. That's another mood, another situation.

YOUNG MAN: (screams) No, no! You want to upset me. I don't know why, but you want to upset me!

USHER: (complacent) God save me!

YOUNG MAN: (with effort) But you haven't . . . succeeded.

USHER: (laughs) It's not easy to upset people!

YOUNG MAN: What did you think? (smiles, with difficulty) Now . . . tell me the truth.

USHER: The walls will fall in on you. It's our custom to make it happen at midnight. Ill-fated hour, nuptial hour. You're going to discover if it's one, if it's the other, if it's both at once.

YOUNG MAN: You can't tell me this so calmly! You can't demand my wallet, my key ring, in order to tell me news that's so . . . !

USHER: So . . . what?

YOUNG MAN: So atrocious!

USHER: (sits, slaps his thigh) Hah! What an arbitrary interpretation! Maybe I should solicit just retribution from you! All I did was tell it like it is. What a mess! You were crying out for the news. Good, bad, you didn't care. What do I know? It could be good news. What were you before? An office worker. Not everyone has the luck to die crushed, flattened.

YOUNG MAN: You can't tell me news like this. What have I done? Are you crazy?

USHER: Mister, what do you want me to tell you? You make a drama out of everything. All I did was give you a confidential piece of news, and you're going on and on about it forever.

YOUNG MAN: The room got smaller, but that can happen . . . It's not so horrible!

USHER: No, it isn't.

YOUNG MAN: Right? We're not in a country full of madmen. The room didn't get smaller. (a childish smile) The wine.

USHER: That's it.

YOUNG MAN: I got confused. Then I stopped counting. The room stopped moving. No one makes the world move. It's like always, intact.

USHER: But you're wrong, mister. They are making your room move!

YOUNG MAN: (corrects himself, screaming) The walls! It's the walls! (frozen) No, no. You're lying to me.

USHER: (observes him. Then after a silence, laughs.) Why not? I'm lying, I'm not lying, what difference does it make to you? It makes you scream to high heaven?

YOUNG MAN: (screaming) It makes a big difference. It makes me nervous! Leave me in peace! You fluster me! You . . . !

USHER: (festive) So you're angry! Finally you're angry! I was joking! We were so glad when you stopped pestering us about your room! We worried about your health. That's why we went for the doll, or, as the Functionary says, for art. To distract you or . . . (an ambiguous silence)

YOUNG MAN: Is that why you're lying to me now? To distract me, to test me?

USHER: Yes.

YOUNG MAN: I'm in my right mind. I won't pay attention to you.

USHER: (laughs) You were afraid of me! "Truth died." (a pause) The painting is still in good shape.

YOUNG MAN: Where?

USHER: In the other room. Also a young man. He liked the painting. We always use the same one.

YOUNG MAN: The Functionary chose it for me, in the basement.

USHER: You're raving! Do you imagine we're going to have a painting for each one? And when the walls fall down?

YOUNG MAN: Don't dredge that up again, it's stupid!

USHER: Excuse me, it's the custom.

YOUNG MAN: And the curtains? Are the curtains also there, in the other room?

USHER: Of course.

YOUNG MAN: Is my watch there?

USHER: I thought we'd cleared that up. Hadn't you lost it?

YOUNG MAN: I don't know. Maybe it's there and you don't know it. Maybe it was stolen by the young man who occupied my room.

USHER: (charmed by the idea) Yes, yes. Brilliant deduction! Why didn't we think of it before? There's always a third party to blame.

YOUNG MAN: (obstinate) Perhaps at this very moment he's checking the time. You didn't by chance see my watch in his hands?

USHER: I think I did. When he put it in his pocket. (softly) What nonsense!

YOUNG MAN: (with concentrated fury) When I get out of here, I'll punch in his teeth.

USHER: I approve. Get even.

YOUNG MAN: Sunday I'm going to the country.

USHER: Me too! We're like brothers!

YOUNG MAN: I've got to relax for a day. Monday I go back to work. I hope there's no problem.

USHER: Don't worry. The Functionary will give you a reference. He knows everyone. Speaking of the Functionary, I'm leaving. I don't want him to accuse me of meddling. (goes toward the door) Has he got a temper! Like the plague!

YOUNG MAN: Listen to me! You . . . you promised to tell me some news.

USHER: (stops, negligently) I told you lots of news!

YOUNG MAN: Were you lying to me?

USHER: Of course! "Truth is suspect." (laughs)

YOUNG MAN: (with stubborn resolve) Sunday I'm going to the country.

USHER: Very good. No objection. But from here to Sunday there's still a few days. (amused) You can't wait on your feet, in any case. Come here, sit down. (He draws a chair close. Docile, the YOUNG MAN sits. On a sudden inspiration, the USHER puts the doll in his arms. Contemplates him, smiling.) There, you be good and wait. Sunday you'll go to the country, remember. Stay calm, don't move. Wait, wait, wait . . .

(Saying this, he exits, smoothly, furtively, with the same amused smile. The door remains open. The YOUNG MAN looks toward the door, then, with obedient determination, very rigid, the doll in his arms, his eyes unbelieving and stupidly open, he waits.)

Curtain

Translator's Notes

1. The novel in question is Anthony Hope's *The Prisoner of Zenda*.

2. The historical Anne Ninon de Lenclos (1620–1705) was a French lady of fashion, renowned for her beauty, epicurean ways, and extraordinary salon, attended by Richelieu, St. Evremond, La Rochefoucauld, Condé, and Sévigné, among others. In her later years, she was a friend of Madame de Maintenon and Madame de Lafayette.

Information for Foreigners

A Chronicle in Twenty Scenes

Characters

Guides, number contingent
  on number of audience
  groups
Voices, heard at intervals
  throughout

Man in room

Girl, with wet clothes
Man, with pistol

Coordinator
Mature Man, Teacher
Young Man, Pupil

Mother
Father

Group of Men, attack man in
  audience
Man, defends attacked man

Someone from the Audience,
  number contingent on
  number of audience groups
Usherette

Three Men, carry table
Group of Men, surround Girl
Two Workmen

Mother (Sara Palacio de
  Verdt)

Father (Marcelo Verdt)
Two Children (Verdt girl and
  boy)
Chief
Two Policemen

Man in loincloth

Man (Roberto Quieto)
Neighbor #1
Neighbor #2
First Group of Men, tied
  together
Neighbor #3
Second Group of Men, tied
  together
Official
Judge
Guard

Girl, with long hair
  (Hermenegilda)
Four Men, on skates
Husband of Hermenegilda
Mother of Hermenegilda
Neighbors

Man (Juan Pablo Maestre)
Woman (Mirta Elena
  Misetich)
Two Policemen

Group of Policemen, dressed
 as sweepers

Game Players
Policemen, with clubs

Actor #1
Two Men, in box

Actress #1
Actress #2
Actor #2
Policeman #1
Policeman #2

Child-Monster
Children, play Anton Pirulero
First Man

Second Man
Third Man
Young Woman

Two Guards
Prisoners
Visitors to Prison
Pretty Girl
Group of Guards, attack
 Pretty Girl
Little Old Lady
Outlandish-Looking Prisoner

Prostitutes
Man #1
Man #2
Man #3
Man #4

The theater space can be a spacious, residential house, prefera-
 bly two stories, with corridors and empty rooms, some of
 which interconnect. A larger space is needed for the final
 scene.

Situated in the passageways, propped against the walls, are two
 or three vertical rectangular boxes, each with a door and air
 holes.

In a different area, chosen by the director, sits an additional
 box, larger but otherwise the same as those in the passageways.

Some of the corridors are dark, while others, in obvious con-
 trast, are crudely lit.

The audience will be divided into groups, the number and size
 of which will depend on the space. A particular number or
 color can serve to identify each group.

Group 1 will mark one possible development of the action.

Guides 1, 2, 3, 4, etc., lead their respective groups. The order in which the scenes are observed by these groups is left to the director's discretion until the last scene, scene 20, when all groups converge.

In certain scenes, actors play audience members and are actually part of the audience. Audience members, however, are never forced to participate in the action.

The groups cross in the passageways and may watch the same scene—perhaps one taking place in the passageway—when the director considers it necessary.

Excerpts introduced by the guides as "Explanation: For Foreigners" come from Argentine newspapers of the period 1971–72.

GUIDES: Organize the groups.

GUIDE: Ladies and gentlemen: Admission is ———, for adults. If you've already paid, you can't repent. The cost is already incurred. Better to enjoy yourself. No one under eighteen will be admitted. Or under thirty-five or over thirty-six. Everyone else can attend with no problem. No obscenity or strong words. The play speaks to our way of life: Argentine, Western, and Christian. We are in 1971. I ask that you stay together and remain silent. Careful on the stairs.

Scene 1

The GUIDE leads the group toward one of the rooms. The room is completely in shadow. The door closes. We hear a shrill, metallic signal. Then, we hear many voices, indistinct and juxtaposed, carrying on an incomprehensible conversation.

GUIDE: One moment . . . I don't find my flashlight. Remember, opportunity makes the thief. Watch your pocketbooks! (Light comes up on a dark and wrinkled wall.) Only the naked walls are left. (The light travels. A man is seated on a chair, wearing only faded underwear. He raises his head, surprised and frightened. He covers his sex with his hands. To the audience.) Excuse me. I've got the wrong room.

Scene 2

The GUIDE, lighting the way with his flashlight, leads the group out of the room. He tries to open the door of another room. Behind the door a sweet voice sings.

VOICE:

> "Carnation, sleep and dream,
> the horse won't drink from the stream . . ."[1]

GUIDE: (shrugging his shoulders, turns to the group) It's locked. (He knocks. Nicely.) May I? I've brought a group of spectators. And they're getting anxious.

VOICE: (very rudely) What's it to me? Beat it! I'm rehearsing.

Scene 3

GUIDE: (to the group) Sorry. People should be brought up better, don't you think? (tries the latch on the next door. It gives.) Good. Here. Go ahead. (The group enters this other dark room. Against the wall, some chairs. The GUIDE shines his light on them. Then, nicely.) You can position yourselves wherever you like. There are chairs for everyone. (He looks.) No, not enough to go around. (arranges them, offers) Ladies first . . . !

(Lights on in the middle of the room. A young GIRL sits on a chair wearing clothes that are soaking wet. A MAN stands next to her, observing her with a tender smile. The GUIDE waits for people to get comfortable, points out places. Then, with a finger on his lips, he signals for silence and turns, like one more spectator, toward the characters who begin the action.)

MAN: (always speaks softly, tenderly) Why didn't you dry yourself? You're getting the floor all wet. (He bends down and dries the floor with a rag.) Lucky it's not waxed. (The GIRL shivers with cold. The MAN takes off his jacket, puts it on her shoulders. The GIRL looks at it, wraps herself in the jacket.) Why didn't you dry yourself? Wasn't there a towel?

GIRL: No.

MAN: (drying the floor) What a mess! They fill the tub but don't put any towels. What about the water? Was it warm? (The GIRL doesn't answer. He shakes her, gently.) Was it warm?

GIRL: No.

MAN: (He pulls a pistol from his belt and cleans it with a rag.) Ah! This department isn't worth shi . . . (The GUIDE says something. The MAN shoots him a quick look.) Right. (He shows her his weapon.) Do you like it? It isn't loaded. (She looks at it but doesn't answer. The MAN begins loading the gun.) Why so sad? (points to the group) Nothing will happen to you. There are lots of people. They're watching us. (puts the pistol back in his belt) You're not pretty with your hair all wet. But that's not too serious. (He leans toward her, curious.) Tell me, do you dye your hair? (still studying her) You're getting my jacket all wet. Sorry, it's the only one I have . . . (He takes it gently, shakes it, and puts it on. With a shiver.) It's damp. (pointing to the pistol) Do you want it?

GIRL: No.

MAN: I'm leaving it for you. I have another. The jacket I can't, I swear to you.

GIRL: (shaking her head) No.

MAN: (surreptitiously) Speak up! They can't hear a thing!

GUIDE: Louder! Louder!

MAN: What did I tell you? (The GIRL doesn't answer.) Look at me. (She obeys. He holds out the gun.) Take it!

GIRL: No . . . I don't want to.

MAN: Why are you squeezing your legs together? Do you want to go to the bathroom?

GIRL: (nods her head) Yes.

MAN: Then go!

GIRL: They're . . . watching me.

MAN: So? We're all adults, aren't we? They at least are watching. What are you doing, always looking over there? What do you see that's so pretty? (puts his cheek against hers. Looks in the same direction.) Nothing! (separates from her) I like to see people's eyes when I talk to them. (Gently, he turns her head.) Look at me. (He points to the pistol.) Do you want it?

GIRL: No, no! Leave me alone!

MAN: (anxious) Would you like some stockings? (He puts his hand on her foot.)

GIRL: No!

MAN: Always no! Why? My intentions are good. Take it. Don't you get bored all alone? (insists) Take it, it doesn't bite. But don't squeeze the trigger. Unless . . .

GIRL: (barely audible) Unless . . .

MAN: If you squeeze, it's all over. Do you have a boyfriend?

GIRL: No.

MAN: Well then? Take it! I'm leaving it here, on the floor. All you have to do is lean down.

GIRL: For what? I don't want . . . to lean down, I don't want . . . anything.

MAN: The heart and the forehead . . . are sure. I mean, so you don't suffer . . .

GIRL: No . . .

MAN: (caresses her cheek) Of course, no. There's a sun outside. It's hot as hell. So you don't have a boyfriend? Well then . . . ? (He goes toward the door. Turns. Smiles.) I'm going to tell them to heat the water! (He goes out. The GIRL looks at the pistol on the floor, leans down, trembling, stretches her hand. Freezes in the act.)

GUIDE: Ladies and gentlemen, if it bothers you. (He opens the door. Leading the group into the hallway, he explains.) In March 1970, at the Max Planck Institute in Munich, Germany, they began an interesting experiment. Careful on the stairs.

Scene 4

The group enters a white room that adjoins another, also painted white, but that may be smaller. In the first room, a small table with a cage full of white rats. On another table, a metal box outfitted with buttons and a microphone. Carefully folded on an ordinary chair, a white coat.

Through the half-open door one can see in the other room a chair whose armrests are outfitted with side straps attached to electric cables. Cables to tie down a person's legs. A microphone hangs down from the ceiling.

In the first room are the COORDINATOR, dressed in a white coat, and two others in street clothes, a MATURE MAN and a YOUNG MAN. The MATURE MAN lingers in front of the cage, putting his fingers through the bars. trying to attract the rats and get them to play.

COORDINATOR: (to the group, in a professional tone) Gentlemen: The subject of our experiment is to determine the pedagogical effect of punishment. To what degree does punishment accelerate the learning process? Imagine. If with one slap a child learns to behave, we waste years teaching and persuading only with nice words. We don't have time to lose. Soon he will be an adult; soon he will be molded. Molded for destruction, when one slap, two or three electrical jolts at the right moment could put things in place. (He begins observing the MATURE MAN playing with the rats.) The gentlemen will help us to clarify . . . unclear . . . details . . . Please, sir, stop pestering those rats! Idiot! (He goes toward him and kicks him away from the cage.)

MATURE MAN: Okay, okay. I'm sorry. They're so cute that . . .

COORDINATOR: (calm) Of course they're cute. (becoming irritated) Shall we begin?

MATURE MAN: At your orders, sir!

COORDINATOR: (happy) One kick . . . and acquiescence. You, sir, emotionally more mature, will be the teacher.

MATURE MAN: Yes, delighted.

COORDINATOR: (to the YOUNG MAN) You will be the pupil.

YOUNG MAN: (He speaks with a metallic voice, like a parrot.) I will be the pupil.

GUIDE: (to the group, surreptitiously) Everyone's a researcher, even the mule.

COORDINATOR: (drily) Silence! (He takes money and some papers out of his pocket.) Help yourself. Twenty-five marks, or thirty-six dollars for your trouble. If you would be so kind as to sign the receipt and the release. (They sign, take their money. The COORDINATOR hands the TEACHER a white coat.) This is for you. (Cordially, the COORDINATOR helps him on with the coat, adjusts the collar.) There, now. Right this way, please. (He leads them into the other room. The GUIDE follows with his group. COORDINATOR to the PUPIL.) Please be seated. Don't be afraid, it's an experiment, remember that.

PUPIL:

> Happy to please
> I sit with the greatest of ease!

COORDINATOR: I made a mistake. Take off your jacket, roll up your sleeves. (The PUPIL does so.) Thank you. We have to strap you in. If you would like to resign . . .

PUPIL:

> No! For the sake of science
> Let us commence!

COORDINATOR: (strapping him. To the TEACHER.) Will you help me?

TEACHER: (with dispatch) Yes, of course!

COORDINATOR: (From a pocket of his coat, he takes a tube of cream and starts smearing the PUPIL's forearms.) The cream facilitates the passage of current and prevents burns. (winking at him) It's an experiment, don't be frightened. It's like . . . talking to hear yourself talk.

PUPIL:

> I'm not afraid
> I'm not afraid
> I really feel I have it made.

COORDINATOR: (attaches electrodes to the PUPIL's forearms. The TEACHER helps diligently.) How obliging! Thank you.

PUPIL: It's . . . very tight.

COORDINATOR: Let's loosen this a bit. (He does.) You—the Teacher—are going to station yourself at the microphone in the next room. (to the PUPIL) You pay attention. He will read out a group of words, such as *day-sun, night-moon, mother-love,* etc. Then he will repeat the word *day* followed by four others. You must remember which of these four words was associated with *day.* If you make a mistake, you'll receive an electric shock as punishment.

TEACHER: And then you'll learn.

PUPIL: Why will punishment teach me?

COORDINATOR: The shock won't be strong.

TEACHER: Never?

COORDINATOR: No! Unless he really blunders. But it's impossible. They're very obvious associations. For idiots. (to the TEACHER) Let's go! (They go into the adjoining room. The GUIDE settles his group. The COORDINATOR hands the TEACHER a sheet of paper.) Here is the list of words. A clean game: read slowly, with good pronunciation. Wait! Roll up your sleeve.

TEACHER: Me? What for?

COORDINATOR: I want to give you a charge of forty-five volts.

TEACHER: (surprised) Me? I'm the teacher!

COORDINATOR: Don't be afraid. I'm doing it so that you'll appreciate the intensity of the punishment. Otherwise, you might have a heavy hand. (He puts an electrode on the TEACHER's arm, pushes a button.)

TEACHER: (jumps, frightened) That's strong!

COORDINATOR: No, no. You'll start with fifteen volts. You won't have to increase it much. Be seated. Read. Slowly, in a clear voice.

TEACHER: (He sits in front of the metal box, clears his throat, reads haltingly.) Day-sun, night-moon, mother-love, water-ship, plague-war, house-forest, child-innocence, prison-bars, window-freedom, blue-sky, bird-flight, nation-Germany, torture-dissuasion. (He finishes, looks at the COORDINATOR like a child awaiting instructions.)

COORDINATOR: (claps him on the shoulder) Very good! Now you must read one word, then four more, so that the pupil will pick the correct association. If he makes a mistake, say "Error," press the first button, and tell the pupil the voltage with which you're punishing him. Then read the right answer. Punishments start at 15 volts and end at 450. (He makes a horizontal gesture with his hand.) As you see, it couldn't be easier. Begin.

TEACHER: (clears his throat) Sun! Day, forest, mother, water.

VOICE OF THE PUPIL: Day!

COORDINATOR: Very good! (encouraging the TEACHER) Let's go on! Do you like it?

TEACHER: (like a child) Yes! It's terrific!

COORDINATOR: Continue.

TEACHER: Night! Plague, forest, moon, child.

VOICE OF THE PUPIL: Moon!

TEACHER: (enthused) Correct! (to the COORDINATOR, laughing) This is like a drug!

COORDINATOR: Ssshh! Go on!

TEACHER: Mother! Day, water, child, love. (silence from the PUPIL) But this is bread in your belly! What memories do you have of your mother?

COORDINATOR: (with bonhomie) Now, don't help! It's not scientific!

VOICE OF THE PUPIL: Chi . . .

TEACHER: (advises) No!

COORDINATOR: (drily) Excuse me, sir. This is an experiment, not a game.

VOICE OF THE PUPIL: We can't repeat? (the TEACHER looks at the COORDINATOR.)

COORDINATOR: Just this once. You've got to follow the rules.

TEACHER: Just this once, not again. Mother: day, water, child, love. (silence from the PUPIL) Well?

VOICE OF THE PUPIL: Love!

TEACHER: Very good! But faster. (The COORDINATOR nods approval.) Blue: ship, bird, sky, house. (silence from the PUPIL) I'm waiting.

VOICE OF THE PUPIL: Want to repeat?

TEACHER: I won't repeat. How can you not remember? What a fool. (looks at the COORDINATOR, who assents) Answer, I won't wait any longer.

VOICE OF THE PUPIL: Bird!

TEACHER: (pleased) He made a mistake! Now what do I do?

COORDINATOR: (He points to the box. The TEACHER vacillates in his choice among the buttons.) The first. Fifteen volts.

TEACHER: (smiles timidly. Pushes the button.) Here we go! Take that. (Through the door, we see that the PUPIL is jolted but cries out more in surprise than pain. His cries are always in a parrot-voice, stereotyped like those of someone who, as a joke, coarsely imitates moans, groans, and pain. To the COORDINATOR.) I didn't do anything! (into the microphone) Now remember. (He reads.) Plague: child, innocence, love, night.

COORDINATOR: (very low) You forgot war.

TEACHER: I did?

COORDINATOR: Plague-war. It's all right, let it go. It doesn't matter.

TEACHER: (low) Should I repeat? (The COORDINATOR shrugs.) Well? (The PUPIL is silent.) Come on. Quick. Otherwise it's boring, I get tired.

VOICE OF THE PUPIL: Night.

TEACHER: (pleased) He made a mistake! Thirty volts! (instantly presses the second button. A louder groan from the PUPIL.) Moving right along. Child: love, mother, innocence, bird.

VOICE OF THE PUPIL: (quickly) Love!

TEACHER: He made a mistake! You were dreaming! Forty-five volts! (He pushes another button. Howling loudly, the PUPIL arches his back. Surprised by the howling, the TEACHER looks into the other room. To the COORDINATOR, disturbed.) A bit strong, wasn't it?

COORDINATOR: (soothingly) No. This is a scientific experiment, and I am in charge. What experiment? Just as I told you: simply to determine the effectiveness of punishment in learning. If from the beginning we doubt, we'll never arrive at a conclusion.

TEACHER: Yes, that's right. The associations are easy.

COORDINATOR: And it's not so much. I gave you forty-five volts, remember?

TEACHER: I didn't shout. What a weakling! (to the PUPIL) Listen to me. Don't scream. Pay attention. Sky: mother, child, innocence, blue.

VOICE OF THE PUPIL: Blue!

TEACHER: Goooood!

COORDINATOR: Magnificent. We're already getting results.

TEACHER: It's no time to stop, then. Plague: prison, house, forest, war. Well? (Slowly, the COORDINATOR closes the door connecting the rooms.) Repeat. (The COORDINATOR shakes his head.) I can't. (silence from the PUPIL) Well? (to the COORDINATOR) Can I repeat? Just this once. He's not very intelligent. (The COORDINATOR snorts, accedes with a gesture.)

TEACHER: Listen. Don't let your mind wander. Plague: prison, house, forest, war.

VOICE OF THE PUPIL: Prison.

TEACHER: He's an idiot!

COORDINATOR: (exasperated) You must say, "Error," and press the button. That is your job! Save the commentary!

TEACHER: And now he's growling at me! (He presses the button.)

VOICE OF THE PUPIL: (screams)

> No, no! I didn't think
> I'd be in so much pain!

TEACHER: A smart aleck! Well, he better hold up! (into the microphone) Pupil: Pay attention. You think I like pushing these little buttons? Try to remember. Blue: bird, flight, sky, freedom. (waits, nervous) Out with it!

VOICE OF THE PUPIL: I don't remember!

TEACHER: How can you not remember?

VOICE OF THE PUPIL: I don't!

TEACHER: (furious, pushes the button) If you don't remember, take this!

VOICE OF THE PUPIL: (a scream) Sky! (He whimpers.)

TEACHER: Very good! (He wipes the sweat from his face.) You see? With a little determination, you hit it! Okay! Here we go. Flight: bird, blue, forest, night. You gotta be quick. Answer.

VOICE OF THE PUPIL:

I won't play!
No matter what you say!

COORDINATOR: Youth today! Now he refuses!

TEACHER: What's the matter with him? He's howling.

COORDINATOR: He signed the release. He can't give up. The results are important, aren't they? You're not screaming. You can be counted on.

TEACHER: Pupil? Pay attention. I am going to read you the words.

VOICE OF THE PUPIL: Go to hell! Let's change places!

TEACHER: Change places? That's crazy. It'll be worse for you, if you don't answer. Bird: flight, blue, plague, war. And I'm repeating the words. And it isn't allowed! Who do you think you are? Answer!

VOICE OF THE PUPIL: I'll make a mistake!

TEACHER: Answer! (He pushes the button. A scream. To CO-ORDINATOR.) He's screaming.

COORDINATOR: He feels a bit jolted. You have just one thing to watch out for: 450 volts—kaput. Otherwise, after a week, there isn't a mark.

TEACHER: Listen good. Are you listening?

VOICE OF THE PUPIL: Are you listening?

TEACHER: We'll see who's listening. Bird: night, flight, house, plague.

VOICE OF THE PUPIL: I don't remember!

TEACHER: Don't be such an ass!

VOICE OF THE PUPIL: Don't be such an ass! Plague!

TEACHER: (furious) Imbecile! Bird-plague! (to the COORDINATOR) See how he answers! (The COORDINATOR, understanding, shrugs his shoulders.) He's jerking me around! (He pushes a button. The PUPIL screams, weeps. Disconcerted, to the CO-ORDINATOR.) And now he's crying! What do I do?

COORDINATOR: Keep going. Don't worry about it.

TEACHER: Listen, kid, answer right, or I'll blow you away. Window: prison, flight, torture, fr . . . freedom.

VOICE OF THE PUPIL: Torture! Torture!

TEACHER: What did you say? Tortoise! Idiot! You're making fun of me! (He pushes the button. The PUPIL howls.)

COORDINATOR: (checking) One hundred eighty volts. (smiles approvingly) It's moving right along.

VOICE OF THE PUPIL: Let me go, you're hurting me! Oh, my belly!

TEACHER: Do we stop?

COORDINATOR: No.

TEACHER: He doesn't remember anything!

COORDINATOR: He'll remember now.

TEACHER: You think so? He burst into tears. If he doesn't answer, this is useless!

COORDINATOR: It isn't useless! If we don't succeed in getting concrete results, all this suffering will be useless. Besides, you have to.

TEACHER: *I* do?

COORDINATOR: Of course. The tears, the screams. Think about it.

TEACHER: I'm not exactly sucking my thumb!

COORDINATOR: Of course not. Go ahead.

TEACHER: Nation: prison, bars, Germany, torture.

VOICE OF THE PUPIL: I don't know!

TEACHER: (his finger on the button) Out with it!

VOICE OF THE PUPIL: Argentina!

TEACHER: (beside himself) Germany, idiot! (He pushes the button. The PUPIL howls.)

COORDINATOR: Planck Institute, Munich.

TEACHER: (furious) Prison: nation, plague, war, bars.

VOICE OF THE PUPIL:

> I don't know, let me go!
> I want to go home!

TEACHER: (screams) Out with it!

VOICE OF THE PUPIL: Nation!

TEACHER: You made a mistake! (He pushes button after button. The PUPIL howls.)

COORDINATOR: (stops him) Slow! One at a time.

TEACHER: He's fucking with me! Why doesn't he answer right?

COORDINATOR: Make him.

TEACHER: I don't like doing this to you. Is that clear? You signed. Don't count your lost sheep. Concentrate! Here's another. Do you hear me? (silence) Do you hear?

VOICE OF THE PUPIL: (lifeless) Vultures fly near . . .

TEACHER: Moon: night, prison, window, flight. (to the COORDINATOR) He'll get this one. It's easy. (low) If he doesn't answer, what do I do?

COORDINATOR: (gently) I told you.

TEACHER: (puts his hand on the last button. Closes his eyes.) He doesn't answer. Why doesn't he answer?

COORDINATOR: (softly) Laziness. Low level.

TEACHER: Moon.

VOICE OF THE PUPIL: Ni . . . Niii . . . ght . . .

TEACHER: (without consulting the list) He made a mistake. He made a mistake . . . again. (He opens his eyes.) It's deliberate. He can't not know. Still . . . it hurts me . . . (He slowly pushes the last button on the box. Silence. He smiles with relief.) He didn't scream.

COORDINATOR: No. (changes his tone. Exultantly.) Very good! Four hundred fifty volts! Excellent! Your help has been invaluable.

TEACHER: Why didn't he help?

COORDINATOR: Look . . . we choose the risks we take! Sometimes we're not so lucky. (removes the TEACHER's lab coat)

TEACHER: It was his fault. Wasn't it?

COORDINATOR: Yes, yes. Your work was magnificent!

TEACHER: He didn't even make an effort. A baby at the breast could have answered right. Some people like to fuck with you!

COORDINATOR: Yes, yes! You were splendid. (He shakes his hand.) Thank you ever so much. Don't worry. An unforgettable performance.

TEACHER: (flattered) It was nothing. I did what I could!

COORDINATOR: (seeing him to the door) No, no, you were quick, concise, sure. Thanks ever so much! (Again he shakes his hand. The TEACHER exits. The COORDINATOR turns toward the audience, professional.) This experiment, with recorded screams and simulated tortures, was repeated 180 times. Unfortunately, this teacher who continued his punishments to the lethal 450 volts was no exception. Eighty-five percent of the teachers proceeded in the same way. The same test was done in 1960 in the United States. The results? Sixty-six percent. They were obeying rules and weren't responsible. Curious, isn't it? Surprised?

GUIDE: Okay, enough. Don't wear out the audience. (to his group) The experiment was done in Germany and the United States.[2] Here among ourselves, it would be unthinkable, absurd. Ladies and gentlemen, let's look for something more amusing. (He leads his group out of the room.) This way, this way. If you would be so kind . . . Ladies and gentlemen . . .

Scene 5

The GUIDE leads the group to the room that in scene 2 was locked.
GUIDE: (He knocks.) May I?

VERY SILLY VOICE: (from inside the room) Yeeeess.

(The group enters the room. Seated on a chair is a woman made up like a doll, wearing a white dress that reaches to her feet and holding a baby in her arms. The baby, swaddled in tulle and lace, is obviously a doll. Sitting on the floor, at the woman's feet, a young man watches them with an enraptured expression. The group is enveloped in a beam of rosy light. The acting is frankly crude.)

GUIDE: (pleased) Ah! Finally something coherent!

MOTHER: (rocking the child)

> "My rose, asleep now lie
> the horse is starting to cry
> His poor hooves were . . ."[3]

GUIDE: What a picture! (to his group) Make yourselves comfortable. Can you see? Madam . . . (helps her get comfortable. Then, rapidly, drily.) Explanation: For Foreigners. Seven P.M., Wednesday, December 16, 1970. Nestor Martins, attorney, defender of political prisoners and trade unions, consults with his client Nildo Zenteno.[4] They take leave of one another in the street. Six men surround Martins, violently force him into a white Peugeot. Nildo Zenteno rushes back, manages momentarily to free the lawyer. A karate chop to the back of his neck brings Zenteno down as well. The car speeds off. A black Chevrolet escorts it. That car had pulled out of a nearby parking lot of the Federal Police. *Desaparecidos*. (from newspaper) Nestor Martins, thirty-three. Nildo Zenteno, thirty-seven.

MOTHER:

> ". . . bleeding,
> his long mane was frozen,
> and deep in his eyes
> stuck a silvery dagger."

(She suddenly stops. Distorting her voice as though she were a ventriloquist speaking for the little one.) Stop it, Mama. That's old. Daddy, tell me a story.

FATHER: (very sweet) Yes, darling.

MOTHER: (idiotic voice) Daddy, it has to be modern! No morals, Daddy!

FATHER: Yes, darling.

MOTHER: (impatient) Come on, Daddy, start!

FATHER: (enraptured) Precious!

MOTHER: (in the voice of a ferocious little child) I know I'm precious! Why do you go round and around, Daddy?

FATHER: Now, now . . . This child is in such a hurry! Daddy has to think!

MOTHER: Enough horsing around, Daddy. Well?

FATHER: (laughs confusedly. Then, grossly exaggerating the traditional tone in which one tells a story.) Once upon a time . . .

MOTHER: (in the voice of a fierce, exasperated little child) Yeeeess . . .

FATHER: (in the same tone) Once upon a time there was a tall man, ugly, ugly, ugly . . . (with disgust) Bolivian. (resuming the story) He had a pile of children. (drily) They procreate a lot. Then they send the kids here.

MOTHER: What happened to the little kids?

FATHER: (sweetly) They were in the street, begging, stealing . . .

MOTHER: And what happened to the tall man?

FATHER: The tall man met another man. This one was a shorty. They talked and talked . . .

MOTHER: (voice of a stupid baby) About what?

FATHER: Well . . . ! Ugly things! And when they were tired of talking, the tall man walked him to his car.

MOTHER: Who?

FATHER: The shorty. The short one was bad, bad. And then, some men came, and since he was bad, they put him in another car to punish him. Because he was bad, bad. And what did the tall man do?

MOTHER: I don't know!

FATHER: He didn't want them to punish him!

MOTHER: Stupid!

FATHER: He ran and ran and hit the good guys. And then, the good guys put him into the car as well.

MOTHER: The good guys took them for a ride! 'Cause they're so good!

FATHER: So very good!

MOTHER: And then what happened, Daddy?

FATHER: Nothing more was ever known!

MOTHER: Yea, yea, yea!

GUIDE: What horrible acting. So sorry. Let's look for something else. (He pushes the people toward the door.) The whole show's not like this. I hope.

MOTHER: (same voice of a stupid baby) Did they punish them a lot, Daddy?

FATHER: Nothing more was ever known!

MOTHER and FATHER: Yea, yea, yea!

GUIDE: (cutting in) Let's go. Let's go, gentlemen. They need at least another month of rehearsal. What dunces!

Scene 6

GUIDE: Let's go upstairs, see if we have better luck. He who searches finds. They say. (The group goes up the stairs, or down, if the preceding scene took place on the upper level. Natural lighting. When the group reaches the landing of the upper level.) No, I made a mistake. I had you climb to the . . . (stops) In vain. Let's go down.

(They go down. Suddenly, a group of men burst in, hurling themselves at a person in the audience who is talking with someone else. This other person is for a second paralyzed with astonishment. Then shouting, he throws himself into the fray.)

MAN: Let him go! Let him go!

(He succeeds in freeing him. The two make it down a few stairs, but the group of men rush them, surround them, and drag them down the stairs. Over the loudspeaker a distressed voice is heard.)

VOICE: My God, why did I run? (Almost instantaneously, the scene breaks out in another place with other characters. The groups may cross at this moment. Again the voice is heard.) My God, why did I run? (The scene is repeated in another spot.) My God, why did I run?

GUIDE: (meanwhile) If we search carefully, we'll find remains in the catacombs. There aren't many, but we can still hope for surprises. Careful please. Don't wander off now. That's it, all together. Careful on the stairs. Look over here! (matter of factly) A brutish people! Yes, we will find remains. Sometimes discoveries come about by chance. (He examines the door to a room. Opens it. The room is lit.) Oh, this one has good light. Imagine, ladies and gentlemen, the faith, the heroism of the first Christians. To pray in these pigsties. It gives me claustrophobia. (He spots a form covered with canvas in a corner, on the floor.) Here's something. Finally! (He draws near.) Stand back a little, ladies and gentlemen. (with curiosity) What is it? (He lifts an edge of the canvas, immediately lets it fall and steps back.) Puah! What a shitty surprise!

VOICE: My God, why did I run?

GUIDE: Sssh! (turns toward the audience, with a big feigned smile, gives the form a kick)

VOICE: My God, why did I run?

(The GUIDE jumps on the form, tramples it, inflamed. In the

doorway to the room, another GUIDE appears. He claps his hands loudly.)

GUIDE #2: Ladies and gentlemen! Please leave. Out, everyone out! Sorry. We have a few like machines without an off button. If you would be so kind as to follow me. (The light in the room fades out.)

Scene 7

GUIDE #2: What was the other one telling you?[5]

SOMEONE FROM THE AUDIENCE: About the catacombs.

GUIDE #2: (glib) Oh, yes! The remains of the first Christians in the catacombs . . . ! Impressive!

(He opens a room. The GIRL from scene 3 is crawling on all fours toward a corner. Weak light on her. The rest of the room is in shadow. The pistol still lies abandoned on the floor.)

GUIDE #2: What do we have here? What is she sniffing at like a dog? (goes closer. Joking, gives her a slap on the rear. Suddenly he changes expression, helps her to get up.) What is this? Composure. Pull yourself together.

GIRL: (lost) He told me to wait. They keep my head underwater, until . . .

GUIDE #2: (interrupts) Who threw water on you? This isn't Carnival. Excuse me, I have to go back to work. (resumes his professional tone. To the group.) The paintings are fantastic, a little deteriorated, but still . . . (He shines a light on the walls.) Jesus, there's nothing! (He sees a graffito in a corner, crouches, shines a light on it.) Gentlemen, come closer! (looks more closely) What kind of filth is this? (stands) Please, ladies, no! Excuse me, but the ladies may not look! (He gestures them away.) Gentlemen, if you like, but . . . (to the GIRL, very surprised.) *You* did this? Your idea of fun? It was a saint's head and they put a . . . (He finishes with an expressive gesture.) Let go, let go of the pencil!

GIRL: No. It wasn't me.

GUIDE #2: (spots the pistol on the floor) What's this? Just a moment, gentlemen. (He picks it up.) How strange!

GIRL: He left it so that, so that . . .

GUIDE #2: So that you could bullshit me. (He raises his arm as though to hit her. Remembers the audience. Smiles.) What negligence. (referring to the gun) I have to take care of everything around here.

GIRL: I'm thirsty.

GUIDE #2: Then you'll pee and be even wetter. (He shines his light on the walls.) There's nothing here either. But I swear there was. And not this filth! (He slaps her skirt.) No way you're a virgin!

GIRL: I'm thirsty.

GUIDE #2: (looking around) Isn't there any water? In the other room, there's a bathtub filled to overflowing.

GIRL: No! No, damn you!

GUIDE #2: What did I tell you? Does anyone understand women? A difficult bunch. As you see, ladies and gentlemen, there's nothing here either. Only the walls. And this filth. (to the GIRL) You weren't getting discouraged, were you? He left you the pistol? How strange. Who am I to . . . ? (He shrugs.) But don't touch it. If you squeeze the trigger, it's all over. The baths and . . . (He smiles.) I'm meddling in something that's none of my business. This is the safety. I'm leaving it up. Careful with the trigger. Sit down.

GIRL: (She sits, shakes her head.) I don't want it.

GUIDE #2: There's no danger, stupid! The slightest touch and it goes off.

GIRL: Take it!

GUIDE #2: (surprised) Why? Soaking and thirsty, it's not a good combination. (He puts the pistol on her lap, takes her hand and places it on the weapon.) Do you have a boyfriend? Touch this and it's all over, done with.

GIRL: I'm thirsty. (She raises her hands.)

GUIDE #2: Right. Sorry. I forgot. Ladies and gentlemen, forgive us for the . . . (He points to the wall.) How mortifying!
If you would be so kind as to follow me . . . (He opens the
door, indicates the exit. At this moment an USHERETTE arrives carrying a tray. She invites the group to have a glass of
wine.) Help yourselves, ladies and gentlemen. It's on the
house. There's no reason to be scared: you won't have to pay
for it. It's all included. Then we'll go on with our visit. (A
scream is heard. To the audience.) Who screamed? Who is
the imbecile who screamed?

Scene 8

The USHERETTE steps close to the GUIDE and whispers a few
words in his ear.

GUIDE: (making amends) Forgive me. In room 3 we are going to
find something interesting. "Finally!" you must be saying to
yourselves. "We should have stayed home." (He laughs.) Ah,
theater's a risky business! What do you think? TV's a better
bet, isn't it? But no, gentlemen. All is not lost. Please, gentlemen. I'm swallowing the "ladies" so I can go faster. With so
many "ladies and gentlemen, ladies and gentlemen," I can't
go on to anything else. (He leads the group through the passageway. The group is shunted aside by three men carrying a
long, half-finished table. It is missing a few strips of wood on
the surface. It is an ordinary table except that it has a strap
nailed to one end. One of the men carries a tool box.) The
first Christians were very persecuted. They were fed to the
lions. (The men put the table on the floor.) Until San Martín.[6] What would the Spanish say about San Martín? "That
son of a bitch traitor. That black shit." (The men start to saw
and drive nails, as though they were alone. They are block-
ing the passageway.) Can't you work somewhere else? (The
men don't answer.) This way, gentlemen. Here's a little path.
(They can't get through. The men move the table, forcing the
group toward the GIRL's room.)

WOMAN'S VOICE:

> "Down he went to the river,
> Oh, down he went down!"[7]

GUIDE: What a pain in the ass she is with that lullabye! (He looks at the door.) Here we are again. We may as well . . . Through here. Sooner or later we'll see a whole scene. (He opens. Joking.) Well? Have you dried yourself? How's . . . (There are some men surrounding the GIRL. The GUIDE quickly closes the door, shoos the people away. With a false smile.) No, I made a mistake. Room 3, they told me. Careful on the stairs. This way, ladies and gentlemen. Ladies, once again. It's nicer . . .

WOMAN'S VOICE:

> "And his blood was running,
> Oh, more than the water."

(The GUIDE snorts. Two men have positioned the table against the wall, clearing the passageway. They are smoking cigarettes, like two workers taking a break.)

GUIDE: (to the workmen) Room 3? This one here? (The men nod yes.) Thank you!

Scene 9

The room is lit with rosy light. Four chairs. There is a group comprising a man, a woman, and two other adults disguised as children, a girl and a boy. Their makeup is exaggerated, and their clothes are cheap, vulgar. The MOTHER is sewing, the FATHER is seated a little apart, and the CHILDREN are playing at throwing a hoop.

On the far side of the room are the CHIEF and two POLICEMEN. They sit very erect with their arms crossed over their chests. The characters act very broadly, a little like marionettes. The tone is grossly exaggerated.

GUIDE: (in a professional tone, dry and rapid) Explanation: For Foreigners. July 2, 1971. Marcelo Verdt and his wife, Sara Palacio de Verdt, were kidnapped by a group of eight men. *Desaparecidos*. Both were members of RAF, Revolutionary Armed Forces.[8] According to information in the newspapers, the wife, before disappearing, brought the children to her sister for protection.

MOTHER: (moving her hand as though sewing) Children, I'm making a little outfit for the one who is best behaved!

CHILDREN: (playing) Thank you, Mommy!

POLICEMEN: (coming forward) Hands up, in the name of the law!

MOTHER: (raising her arm, protecting her face like the heroine in a silent movie) Oh! (The FATHER doesn't move.)

CHILDREN: Mommy, Mommy, who are they?

MOTHER: Don't be afraid, my darlings! No one is hurting your mother!

CHILDREN: Blessed Mommy!

POLICEMAN: (comes close, snatches at her clothes) You're disguised! (shoving her violently)

CHILDREN: Mommy, Mommy, who are they?

POLICEMEN: Where's your husband?

MOTHER: I don't know!

CHILDREN: What do you mean, you don't know, Mommy! In the bathroom! Making caca! (They call.) Daddy! Daddy! They're looking for you!

FATHER: (gets up, comes forward, wide-eyed) Who? What's happening?

POLICEMAN: This is what's happening! It's all over! (screams) Silence everyone! Let's get out of this hole! The car's out front!

MOTHER: Not the children! They don't know anything about it!

POLICEMEN: Them too!

MOTHER: Have pity!

POLICEMEN: Silence! Let's go! Everyone!

(They put the chairs together to make the car. All squeeze in. One of the POLICEMEN holds the hoop between his hands and handles it as though it were a steering wheel. He imitates the sound of a motor. The children wave. The POLICEMAN brakes suddenly. The others fall backward. They get out of the car, their gestures exaggeratedly frightened.)

CHIEF: They fell!

MOTHER: (on her knees) Pity!

POLICEMAN: What should we do with the kids?

CHILDREN: Daddy!

FATHER: (dignified) I'll protect you, don't be afraid. (puts his arms around them)

CHIEF: (to the POLICEMAN) Idiot! Why did you bring the kids?

POLICEMAN: You said everyone, Chief.

MOTHER: They're innocent!

CHIEF: I'll see if they're not already lost. Kids: Who created the flag?

MOTHER: (begging them) Answer right, answer right!

CHILDREN: (In unison) Manuel Belgrano!

CHIEF: When?

CHILDREN: February 27, 1812.

CHIEF: Where?

CHILDREN: On the banks of the Paraná. He had it blessed right there, beneath a blue and white sky, blue and white sky, blue and white . . .

CHIEF: Exactly! Very good! (kisses them) Here's a prize. (gives them each a piece of candy)

CHILDREN: Thank you, sir!

CHIEF: (to the MOTHER) Take them home. And don't be long.

POLICEMAN: Chief, what if she doesn't return?

CHIEF: (with an exaggeratedly sinister laugh, pointing to the FATHER) This one stays here. It's in his interest that she return. (to the MOTHER) Take my advice: be discreet. I'm doing you a favor. Don't be long. Take a taxi.

MOTHER: What are you going to do to him?

CHIEF: Nothing! From his eye to his sex. But only if I'm vexed.

MOTHER: Marcelo!

FATHER: My love!

CHIEF: Take them home. We don't have any small sacks. They're only in the way. Move it.

MOTHER: Come, children! Give Daddy a kiss. (The FATHER kisses them.) Don't be afraid. We're going home.

CHILDREN: (happy) The men are nice, Mama!

MOTHER: (moves off with the CHILDREN. Picks up the outfit she was sewing. To one of them.) Tell Grandma that the hem was turned here.[9] Will you remember?

CHILD: Yes, Mama.

MOTHER: There's soup in the pot. Have it for supper.

CHILDREN: If you're not there, we won't eat any soup! We won't eat any soup!

MOTHER: Be good!

CHILDREN: Where are you going, Mama?

MOTHER: I'm going with Daddy. You behave. (hugs them)

CHILDREN: Mommy! Mommy!

GUIDE: (choked up) It gets to you, doesn't it?

(The MOTHER separates from the CHILDREN and returns toward the CHIEF. During the good-bye scene the POLICEMEN were trying various sacks—as though they were items of clothing—on the FATHER. They have found the right one. Then they take him out of the room.)

CHILDREN: (singing in a round) We won't eat any soup! We won't eat any soup!

MOTHER: Here I am. Where's my husband?

CHIEF: Husband? What husband? Take off your clothes.

GUIDE: (quickly) Let's go! Let's get out of here! (claps his hands) Out! Where's "Carnation, sleep and dream"? Who wants more wine? (pushes the group toward the door) Follow me! Quick! No dawdling! (The group goes out. The GUIDE closes the door, leans against it.) Ouf!

Scene 10

GUIDE: A little wine! Careful . . . on the . . . stairs. (The USHERETTE brings him a glass of water.) Water? For me? What for? (remembers) Oh, right. She's waiting for water! Come, gentlemen, this way. We're almost there. Just another little minute. No reason to fret. (Again they enter the room of the GIRL from scenes 3, 7, and 8. Her clothes are drenched. The GIRL is breathing anxiously. She's seated, with the pistol, which is dry, in her lap. To the group.) Come in. Careful on the stairs. Or rather: fasten your seatbelts, no smoking. (He laughs. To the GIRL, very amiably.) May I? (He puts the glass and the pistol on the floor. Takes the chair on which she is sitting. Offers it to a woman in the audience.) Sit, madam, sit. She may have wet it, but she didn't piss on it! (He dries the chair with a hankie. To the woman.) Please, have a seat! (to the GIRL) They paid admission. Are you thirsty? (The GIRL, lost, doesn't answer. The GUIDE shakes her gently.) Hey! Wake up. I'm asking you if you're thirsty. (The GIRL shakes her head no.) Oh, no? I brought you water. Drink it. (He takes the glass, brings it to her lips. The GIRL resists.) And now, what do I do with the glass? I need my hands free. I'm working. This can't be! Drink, little girl, drink. The water flowed . . . (forcing her) There. There, that's good. So capricious! Well, I don't like people pulling my leg. You're all wet. (puts his hand under her skirt) Even your little fire-cracker. (He laughs. Turns toward the audience.) Oh, excuse me. (takes the pistol) Shall I take it? No? Freedom is within your grasp. No? (He puts the barrel against her breast.) How stupid. I can't. (He cleans the weapon, puts it in the GIRL's lap.) I don't know why they trust you so . . . It's loaded. If you had a boyfriend, old girl . . . But like this. Idiot, why endure so much? (Another GUIDE appears in the doorway.)

OTHER GUIDE: (shouting) What are you doing *here?* It's about to start *there!* And they're giving out wine! It's not to be missed. I saw it! Exceptional! You can understand everything!

GUIDE: Really? Step on it, fellas, let's go! Move it, girls!

OTHER GUIDE: (teases) Don't you mean ladies and gentlemen?

GUIDE: (to OTHER GUIDE) There's wine? For sure? (OTHER GUIDE affirms it and leaves.) If you would be so kind, ladies and gentlemen . . . (He holds open the door so the group can pass through. Before closing the door, in a friendly way.) Think about it, little girl.

Scene 11

In the passageway, one of the vertical wooden boxes.

GUIDE: Wait! This has always intrigued me . . . (tries to see through the peephole) I can't see a thing. How about you, sir? (Someone from the audience has a look.) It's very dark. (He knocks at the door. Jokingly.) Is anyone home? *Hay alguien?* (Curious, he opens the door. There's a heavily made-up man inside, dressed in a loincloth, staring fixedly. Matter of factly.) Hi. (He closes the door, turns toward the audience with an uncomfortable smile. As though it were not so strange.) What a surprise! To me this is very curious . . .

OTHER GUIDE: (shouts from the doorway of the other room) Well? What are you waiting for? A carriage? If you don't get there at the beginning, they won't understand anything!

GUIDE: (annoyed, referring to the vertical box) What about this? Does anyone understand this? (to the OTHER GUIDE) I give the orders in my group! And if they don't get it, too bad for them! This way, gentlemen! (He leads them in the opposite direction.) Follow *me!* (A panting death rattle is heard through the door of a room they pass.)

GUIDE: (He lingers in front of the door, listening to the death rattle inside.) What could this be? (A MAN passes by, whistling.)

MAN: (to GUIDE) Good day!

GUIDE: Good day! (surprised) Well, he's happy! Let's follow him. (referring to the death rattle in the room) Sounds like that and we've really got a mess on our hands! We can check it out later. (He and the group follow the MAN. The MAN walks along, whistling. He meets another man who is coming from the opposite direction.)

MAN: Good day!

NEIGHBOR #1: Hello! How's it going, doctor?

(They shake hands. They continue walking together. The group follows them. They enter a large room, where NEIGHBOR #2 is sweeping the floor. Two chairs stacked in a corner, against the wall.)

NEIGHBOR #2: Hello, doctor!

GUIDE: (to his group) Watch out for the cars! Stay on the sidewalk, please!

(He situates them. He hasn't finished doing so when the FIRST GROUP OF MEN enters at a trot, one behind the other, tied together at their waists.)

FIRST GROUP OF MEN: Let us through! Let us through!

(They come forward, trot through the room, then suddenly halt in front of the MAN and surround him, forming a closed circle.)

MAN: Excuse me.

FIRST GROUP OF MEN: Quieto! Quieto![10]

MAN: Are you calling me? What do you want? (The men accelerate, tightening their circular movement, forming two closed rings.) Excuse me. Let me through.

NEIGHBOR #1: What's going on, doctor?

NEIGHBOR #2: (stops sweeping) Hey! Let him go!

NEIGHBOR #3: (from the audience) What the hell is going on? (comes forward to help the MAN)

MAN: Let me go! Enough fooling around!

(He pushes, tries to get through the circle. Hits, struggles. The men try to drag him toward the door.)

NEIGHBORS: Let him go! Let him go!

(They try to break up the group, NEIGHBOR #2 hitting out with his broom. The SECOND GROUP OF MEN enters, also at a trot and tied together at their waists. They sing.)

SECOND GROUP OF MEN:

> Peace and security
> That is our domain
> With a little authority
> Order will be maintained!

(Observing the tumult, they linger.)

OFFICIAL: (heading the SECOND GROUP OF MEN) What's going on here? This is scandalous! Halt! Separate!

(The fight freezes.)

NEIGHBORS: (all at the same time)
Sir, they were pushing him!
(alternating)
—Over here.
—Over there.
—They tied him up.
—They dragged him down!

OFFICIAL: One at a time, magpies. Who asked you anything? (to the group in the fight) And you, you're prisoners in the name of the law. (He "aims" at them, with his finger. The SECOND GROUP OF MEN "handcuffs" them. They're all, including the MAN, put into a line and tied together at the wrists.)

NEIGHBORS:

>Officer, sir:
>Why the arrest?
>He's one of the best!

OFFICIAL:

>It doesn't matter, my esteemed citizens
>Have faith
>Justice is there for a reason
>To prevent baseness, which is treason.

NEIGHBORS: But we saw . . . !

OFFICIAL:

>What you saw is of no consequence
>If there's offense
>Rest assured
>The man's secure . . .

SECOND GROUP OF MEN: Sure!

(They "take aim" at the NEIGHBORS.)

OFFICIAL: In my providence.

(The NEIGHBORS mix in with the audience. The OFFICIAL moves off to the side, crosses his arms, his expression serious. The FIRST GROUP OF MEN and the MAN attacked in the first place draw near. One of the men from the second group arranges the chairs.)

OFFICIAL: (seating himself. To the MAN.) Name.

MAN: Quieto.

GUIDE: (shouts) Sí, Quieto! (to his group) *Quieto* means quiet. (smiles) Stop a moment. (gestures toward the group) So they'll understand. Otherwise, they'll miss the point. (The others stop the action. In a dry, professional tone.) Explanation: For Foreigners. July 7, 1971. Roberto Quieto, attorney, defender of political prisoners, resists a kidnapping attempt. Fortunately, the neighbors intervene and call a police squad. The kidnappers turn out to be policemen. Dr. Quieto was put at the disposition of the executive power. Subsequently he was accused of having been implicated in an auto theft and of having participated, after his detention, in various subversive acts. He was transferred to Rawson Prison, 730 miles from Buenos Aires. What happened then? I don't remember. Lost in the night of time. (smiles) But he wasn't so innocent. High up in the Montoneros, the son of a b——. It's not my responsibility. Although when you have the truth, I don't know why it should be hidden. Go on. I'm done.

OFFICIAL: (to the MAN) Name.

MAN: Quieto.

OFFICIAL: Quieto! That's what I'm telling *you!* Now what is your name?

MAN: Blame.

OFFICIAL: (suspicious) Ohhhh? (to the FIRST GROUP OF MEN) And you? What are your names?

FIRST GROUP OF MEN: (They sing.)

> Peace and security
> That is our domain
> With a little authority
> Order will be maintained!

SECOND GROUP OF MEN:

> If you're lying
> You'll get bruised!

OFFICIAL:

> Explain what happened
> I'm confused!

FIRST GROUP OF MEN:

> Boca will never lose!
> Boca's the team we choose![11]

OFFICIAL: (very pleased) For this, you are excused. But who began . . .

FIRST GROUP OF MEN: That man!

OFFICIAL: No more rhyming! (to the MAN) Don't you know that it's a crime to incite a riot in the street? (to the SECOND GROUP OF MEN) Did they stop traffic?

SECOND GROUP OF MEN: Yes, sir! They delayed it!

OFFICIAL: For how long?

SECOND GROUP OF MEN: For three minutes!

OFFICIAL: Re-create it!

SECOND GROUP OF MEN:

> In their cars the men grew irritated
> At the office work accumulated.

OFFICIAL: (to the first group, fiercely) I want a confession. (sweetly) What team are you from?

FIRST GROUP OF MEN:

> Boca will never lose
> Boca . . .

OFFICIAL: Fine, fine, no need to repeat! (The FIRST GROUP OF MEN "free" their hands, which had been "cuffed." To the MAN.) What about you?

MAN: What about me?

OFFICIAL: What team are you from?

MAN: I nurse the same illusion.

OFFICIAL: I smell collusion. Why aren't you from San Lorenzo?

MAN: Because I'm not?

OFFICIAL: Don't be a wise guy! (The SECOND GROUP OF MEN hit MAN. To the others.) And you, what are you waiting for? Get going!

MAN: You can't let them go! They attacked me! I want to see my attorney!

OFFICIAL: The one who gives the orders here is me. (to the others) And you, once again, (sweetly) why don't you do your work?

FIRST GROUP OF MEN: (tied together at their waists, they trot out, singing)

> For us it was a sad event
> That ended to our detriment
> Of this our song's a testament!
> For us it was a sad event
> That ended to our detriment
> Of this our song's a testament!

OFFICIAL: (to the MAN) Justice will be done.

(One of the men in the second group puts on a judge's robe and comes closer. Another moves in a chair and has him sit. Becoming the GUARD, he remains standing behind the JUDGE's back.)

JUDGE: (to the MAN) You're free. Being from Boca's no crime. But next time . . .

(The MAN frees his hands and stands up. The JUDGE turns halfway around and grabs him from behind. No sooner has he done so when the GUARD leans into the MAN and pushes him roughly down by the shoulders, forcing him to sit. The MAN again joins his hands as though they were handcuffed.)

OFFICIAL: (to the MAN) You stole a car. Your trial's pending. Your sentence could be unending!

MAN: I need defending!

OFFICIAL: Superintending! (to the JUDGE) He stole a car.

JUDGE: He did not steal a car!

MAN: Am I absolved? Can I go?

JUDGE: Why not? Go ahead!

(He turns so that his back is to the MAN. The previous scene is repeated: the MAN frees his hands, the GUARD forces him to sit down again, etc.)

OFFICIAL: He robbed a bank!

MAN: I was in prison!

JUDGE: (It starts again.) Absolved!

MAN: Thank you. Can I go?

JUDGE: Why not? Go ahead. (again. The rhythm speeds up.)

OFFICIAL: He robbed a station!

JUDGE: (over his shoulder) What kind of station?

OFFICIAL: Service station. Five old wrecks.

MAN: (forced to sit) How? I was in prison!

OFFICIAL: (with pretended fury) Guards, you let him go?

JUDGE: (turns) Why can't you see? There is no case. Let him go free! (turns his back)

OFFICIAL: He robbed a commissary, several stores, and several dairies!

MAN: (forced to sit)

> If I'd been seized
> How could I be eating cheese?

JUDGE:

> He is innocent
> Surely
> I declare it
> Firmly.

MAN: (stands up, etc.) Thank you. Can I go?

JUDGE: Naturally. Why not. (It starts again. The action accelerates to the point of dislocation but always remains precise. The speeches are transferred but not the actions, which remain a constant with each character.)

OFFICIAL: Don't move. I've heard a little story!

JUDGE: He murdered a canary.

MAN:

> That isn't fair!
> I love all canaries
> Everywhere!

OFFICIAL: You love them, but you kill them!

JUDGE: Guards, you let him go?

OFFICIAL:

> Your Honor, you're the witness
> Of this bad faith.

MAN: I only want to live!

JUDGE: Guards, you let him go?

OFFICIAL: If he'd been seized

MAN: How could I've been eating cheese?

JUDGE: Thank you.

OFFICIAL: Beat it! I can't stand you anymore!

MAN: I'm going back to my city!

JUDGE: Can I go?

OFFICIAL: Beat it!

MAN: (resisting those who are making him sit) No, no, I was in prison!

JUDGE: He's free! Oh, such obsession!

OFFICIAL: He's free! What fascination!

MAN: But I'm not!

JUDGE: Yes, you are! So you better shut up! (turns his back, covers his ears)

OFFICIAL:

> Enough already! He's hard to handle.
> All that screaming. What a scandal!

(gestures to the guards to take the MAN away. To the audience.)
The idiots they send me, it's outrageous!

> The courts
> aren't beneficial
> Unless they're
> sacrificial!

(lights out)

GUIDE: Shit! What happened? They turned out the light without telling me! Cretins! (takes out his flashlight, switches it on) Where is the door? Luckily I know the house. (opens door. The passageway is lit.) This way, gentlemen. There aren't any stairs. But be careful all the same. You only get to stumble once, like the tango says. Hey, hey. Everyone make it? (He leads the group through the passageway. They pass the door to the room where the death rattle was heard. It is heard again. The GUIDE puts his ear to the door. Admiringly.) Persistent! We go in? We don't go in? What do you want to do? Free choice. At my orders! We go in!

Scene 13

The GUIDE opens the door. The labored breathing stops. There is a GIRL with long hair laid out on a stretcher, with a sheet carefully folded under her feet.

GUIDE: (advancing on tiptoe) Don't make any noise. She's sleeping. (He approaches, looks at her. The GIRL smiles at him. Sweetly.) How're you doing?

GIRL: (sits up, brushes her hair off her face, folds her hands in her lap. She looks at the group with a semismile. Silence. Then, very simply, colloquially.)

> I would like to die
> as softly as possible
> So that my friends will think
> she is sleeping
> in the earth
> become a worm
> digging in the earth
> so that in spring
> the flowers blossom
> After my death
> I want my children
> to sit at the table
> and say
> at her age
> Mama
> ran off with some guy

What a shame
poor old Dad
staring at the tablecloth
his cup of coffee
searching for her
This is how I want to die
as simply
as though I had never lived
What a lovely thought
to leave like that
not causing any pain
The cup of coffee
that no one drinks
absent . . .

(Silently, a character mixed in with the audience goes up to the GIRL. He puts his hand over her mouth and nose. The GIRL offers desperate, mute resistance. She dies. The man gently lays her out, covers her with the sheet. Then he moves off and mixes in with the crowd, like one more spectator.)

GUIDE: (amazed) How about that? (looks at the man) And now he's so calm! But what a feat! Phenomenal! (He lifts the sheet. Matter of factly.) She's dead. Poor creature! Really, without so much as a moan. Discreet. And in the bloom of youth! (lets the sheet fall) She spoke of children, a husband. We'll have to go find them. Nice news I've got. What a bad deal. (hopefully) Anyone want to go? Of course, for this there are no volunteers. (furious) The son of a bitch. (He goes to the door, leaving the audience.) Excuse me. (He opens the door, yells out.) I need someone from the family! Quick! Someone from the family! (He comes back inside.) She didn't move, did she? What with the advances of medicine, for a moment I thought that . . .

(FOUR MEN enter, two-by-two, each pair moving as one. They are wearing white smocks down to their feet, very loose, belted at the waist. They come in on skates. Their faces are painted with large red smiling mouths. One pair beats pot lids; the other pair waves a white sack.)

FOUR MEN: (singing)

Tachín, tachín, tachín
She died as she would have ordained
Without causing any pain.

GUIDE: What about the family? I've got to tell them . . . It's so
unfortunate . . . My heartfelt sympathy. (extending his hand)

FOUR MEN: (They pay no attention to the GUIDE. They approach the stretcher, lift the sheet. Sing.)

The jokester
Coaxed her

GUIDE: (very confused) Choked her . . . A son of a bitch
who . . . (searches with his eyes. The men start putting the
GIRL into the sack. Surprised.) What are you doing? But . . .

FOUR MEN: (sing)

But nothing
But nothing
Just doing our bit
Ashes to ashes
Shit to shit

GUIDE: (indignant) That's gross! Don't you see there's people?
You must have been raised in a barn! Ladies, your forgive-
ness. I knew nothing . . . The modern theater is like this. No
respect for the ladies!

FOUR MEN:

(They finish putting the GIRL into the sack, leaving her head
out. They tie the end of the sack around her neck. It is evident
that the GIRL is playing dead: though her head is bent over, she
is able to support it. The FOUR MEN hold the bundle, swing it
hammocklike. They sing.)

If you don't like this Tin Pan band
Because it hasn't any flair
Because it just gave you a scare
Swing high, swing well
You can go to hell!

GUIDE: Go on!

FOUR MEN:

> Tachín, tachín, tachín,
> Tachín, tachín, tachín!
> Pran-pran-pran!
> Taratá-ta-ta!

(They near the door. The HUSBAND and MOTHER enter. The HUSBAND is wearing threadbare clothing. His hair is long and all over the place. The MOTHER is the typical little old lady— black clothes, shawl over her head. Both act crudely, like prototypes of desperate people.)

HUSBAND: What happened? I heard screams!

MOTHER: Sirs, have pity! Where is my daughter? Darling! Darling!

GUIDE: Oh my God, the family's here!

MOTHER and HUSBAND: (together) We've come to look for our poor Hermenegilda.

FOUR MEN:

(They come back, set the corpse down; it supports itself against the stretcher. Horrified.)

> That name she inherited
> She certainly merited!

MOTHER and HUSBAND: (together)

> We're here to find out
> What she finally merited!

GUIDE: Oh no! If these two speak in verse, I'm leaving!

> Although the language may be terse,
> I can't bear
> so much pain.

I'm leaving! (He pushes away from the crowd, but upon hearing the HUSBAND, he stops, comes back.)

HUSBAND: Where is she?

FOUR MEN: (They shake the corpse in front of the HUSBAND's face.) We don't know! We don't know! She was never here!

HUSBAND: What do you mean? She came here to buy wine!

FOUR MEN: (They turn the corpse facedown on the stretcher, look underneath.) She bought her bread and went away, evaporated . . . Surely it was fated! (They look at the ceiling. The HUSBAND and MOTHER imitate them. The men point.) Look, sir. That moth . . .

HUSBAND: She wasn't a moth! At dawn . . .

FOUR MEN:

> She was a moth. At dawn
> Before the sun came up full
> we found her eating
> wool

MOTHER: It's not true! She didn't like wool!

FOUR MEN:

> Was she a woman or a moth?
> The question's far from risible.
> Lady, lady don't be miserable.
> Don't be upset
> We'll give you your daughter yet.

(They approach an interior door. They call the HUSBAND and MOTHER as one would a dog.)

Tch, tch, tch . . .

(The HUSBAND and MOTHER advance, their smiles exaggeratedly hopeful. The others open the door. The interior is dark. The HUSBAND and MOTHER look in.)

FOUR MEN:

> You'll find her here, here!
> So be of good cheer, cheer!

(Moving in unison, the FOUR MEN push them inside with kicks in the rump.) And stop mugging! (They close the door. They sway.)

> Ladies, Gentlemen, dearest friends
> Our show is over, Curtains!

(They take the corpse. They lead the way to the exit, singing.)

> Tachín, tachín, tachín!
> Tachín, tachín, tachín!
> Tarará-ta-ta!
> Tarará-ta-ta!

GUIDE: (enthused) Let's go, let's go! Let's follow them! See what happens! They're entertaining! (The group follows the FOUR MEN and GUIDE. The FOUR MEN enter a contiguous room and close the door. An actor, pretending to be part of the audience, opens it. The interior is dark. An enormous club comes out and hits the actor over the head. He falls. The GUIDE leans over him.) Why did he butt in? I'm the Guide here! One to a group! (He pokes him. The man doesn't move. He then lifts him by the armpits and puts him into one of the vertical boxes. He talks all the while, completely dissociated from his actions.) That's how it is. In they all go but . . . who takes the potatoes out of the fire? The son of a bitch. If he was part of the audience, why did he make like an actor? Vanity, vanity will be the end of us all! . . . (He closes the door.) Now what were we going to see?

SOMEONE FROM THE AUDIENCE: The catacombs.

GUIDE: Right. Thank you. The first Christians really had a hard time of it. Just thinking about how the lions loved to chew them up . . . Human meat, they say, is sweet. Sweet, bitter, what could be stupider. (They cross with another group. To the OTHER GUIDE.) Where's there something good? We went in here, and it's all fucked up. (Without stopping, the OTHER GUIDE points to a door.)

The GUIDE leads the group into the designated room. Inside is a group of NEIGHBORS all crowded together, some looking over the heads of others. On the far side, two POLICEMEN crouch, their expressions very attentive. In the center are the MAN and WOMAN, both heavily made-up. Their clothes are cheap, flashy; the WOMAN wears very high heels. All the acting is crude, infantile, and exaggerated.

GUIDE: Attention. Ladies and gentlemen, this is the main course. So they tell me. Hope it's true. Make yourselves comfortable. If you find a chair, be seated. Silence, please. The story of a BM, or bad marriage. (His tone is professional, dry and quick.) Explanation: For Foreigners. On the afternoon of July 13, 1971, Juan Pablo Maestre and his wife, Mirta Elena Misetich, were kidnapped by a group of men. Juan Pablo Maestre managed to run a few yards but then was shot. Mirta Elena Misetich ran in the opposite direction, losing a shoe. She was captured and pushed into one car; her husband was thrown into another. Shortly afterward, a police squad sent to the scene recovered the shoe and ordered the doorman of an apartment building to wash the blood from the pavement. The body of Juan Pablo Maestre appeared days later in Escobar. Of Mirta Elena Misetich there was no further news. Both belonged to the RAF, or Revolutionary Armed Forces. Juan Pablo Maestre, twenty-eight years old. Mirta Elena Misetich, the same age.

MAN: (with a conspiratorial air) Let's plant a bomb here

WOMAN: (with a conspiratorial air) And a bomb over there!

MAN: When these go off

WOMAN: No one will be spared!

MAN and WOMAN: (taking bombs with fuses out from under their clothes)

     Subversion, subversion,
     all rise up!
     in revolution!

MAN: (looking around) Let's go, all clear!

WOMAN: Nothing will be left here! (They take a few cautious steps.)

POLICEMAN: (comes forward, arm extended) Hands up! In the name of the law!

MAN: We're caught! Run! (They drop their bombs and run in opposite directions.)

POLICEMAN: (aims with his finger and shoots) Pum!

(The MAN falls. His blood is obviously fake. The other POLICE-MAN runs after the WOMAN.)

WOMAN: (stops) Darling!

POLICEMAN: Hey, hey! Justice always triumphs! Olé!

(The two POLICEMEN drag the MAN and WOMAN away. The WOMAN loses her shoe. They exit. Slowly, the NEIGHBORS untangle themselves and come forward.)

NEIGHBORS:

> The ass must be judged
> Not broken!

(The two POLICEMEN reenter. The NEIGHBORS immediately re-form their group.)

POLICEMEN:

> Of our respect
> Here's a token![12]

(They're carrying the MAN, dragging him along. The NEIGH-BORS watch, timidly come forward. Romantic music is heard. More POLICEMEN enter, smiling and wearing sweepers' jackets. They swing long-handled brooms, dance as in a musical comedy.)

GROUP OF POLICEMEN: (They sing.)

> We're here to clean!
> We're here to clean!
> The filth is gone

· Your street is clean!
Let mothers pray
let children play
in celebration!

(Smiling, they sweep. They lift the shoe. They sing.)

Little shoe, little shoe
Whom might you belong to?
Why, to Snow White
or to her mother.

GUIDE: What do you mean, fellas! The little lost shoe was
Cinderella's!

POLICEMAN: (emphatically) I say it's Snow White's or her
mother's. (recovering his smile) Whose little shoe is this?
Madam, is it yours? Say yes. A Prince Charming awaits you
in the wings.

GUIDE: No, no! Error! It's the prince, the prince who searches
for the owner of the shoe, not a cop! Didn't you read the
story?

POLICEMAN: Calm down! It's a free interpretation. (smiling)
Doesn't it belong to anyone? Neighbors? (He shows them the
shoe. The NEIGHBORS immediately deny ownership, shaking
their heads in unison.) So we'll look in another neighborhood.
It'll belong to someone. (He repeats, frowning in the GUIDE's
direction.) It's Snow White's or her mother's.

GUIDE: (servile) Yes, of course, her mother's. Well, let's get
going. We can follow you, can't we? (to his group) We'll just
stroll along. If you get tired, let me know.

GROUP OF POLICEMEN: (They go out with the shoe. Asking.)
Madam, is this yours? Is this yours? Young man? (The group
follows them. They enter another room. The WOMAN, wearing no makeup, is seated on a chair. Sitting nearby on the
floor, with her legs crossed, is a GIRL, who may be the same
as the one from scene 13.)

POLICEMAN: (to the WOMAN) Madam, excuse me. We found a
little shoe. Is it yours? Prince Charming will marry you. Cash

in a flash! You'll live in a palace! Let's see. (He puts the shoe on her foot.) She's Cinderella! It fits! Perfect! What luck, old girl! You win! A royal flush! (bows) Princess! My respects! (The WOMAN stares ahead, immobile. Surprised.) Aren't you happy? What's the matter?

WOMAN: My darling!

POLICEMAN: Your darling was stopped by a cop. (The POLICE-MEN exit arm-in-arm, tap dancing.)

WOMAN:

> I was at home, eating my bread. I was
>   making love. I was kissing my children.
> And you will be the only one who knows
> where and how my body was lost,
> how my voice became unstrung
> Only you will know
>   how to know
> the voices of fear and the faces of
>   desperation
> My God, what did the brave ones become?
> I will speak
> Only you will know
> this tongue.

(A shot is heard.)

GUIDE: What's going on? Did you hear that? It was a shot. (looks at the WOMAN and the GIRL) But why so quiet! It's over. Gentlemen, follow me. Did you like that? (He leads his group out of the room.) A bit mixed up, wasn't it? Me . . . well, what do *you* like . . . I'm old-fashioned. I prefer something else. If this was the main course, what will the others be? (They enter the adjoining room. The GIRL of scenes 3, 7, and 8 lies on the floor, shot, the pistol in her hand. The GUIDE looks at her, surprised. Then, matter of factly, pushing them toward the exit.) Oh, sorry! Shall we? The jug may as well go to the fountain as . . . (Happy music is heard.) How about that music! So there is a little happiness in this world! Enough drama! Let's go. Move along. A little gaiety, dammit!

(The poem spoken by the WOMAN was written by Marina, a Greek girl, who was captured and tortured.)

Scene 15

As the group leaves, the music fades and after a few minutes disappears. Through the passageway comes a group holding hands. They sing.)

GAME PLAYERS:
—Martin Fisherman, will you let me pass?
—Pass, pass, but the last one stays with me!

(The group starts playing Martin Fisherman, a singing game somewhat like London Bridge Is Falling Down. Two children make a bridge with their arms; the others run underneath, single file, holding each other by the waist. The line of children sings for permission to pass through; the last one is taken prisoner. In another version, the children making the bridge ask questions. Those who answer correctly pass through; the others do not. Two lines form, one comprising the "free," the other "prisoners." After everyone has had a question, the longer line wins, and the game may start again.)

GUIDE: Ladies and gentlemen, you're welcome to participate. That's not coercion, only if you want to. Grotowsky used to say: The more physical distance, the more spiritual closeness. What nonsense! Don't be afraid to join in, ladies and gentlemen!

(The game continues. Suddenly one of the men forming Martin Fisherman's bridge yells.)

GAME PLAYERS: (alternately)
—I know that one! Don't let him go!
—Me?

(The latter tries to get off the bridge.)

—I know that one! Don't let him go!
—Don't fight!

—Just answer right!

—I don't have to! No!

(He whistles over his shoulder for help. Those in his line start to push. The others shout.)

—Don't push! Hold tight!

—Wait!

(Nevertheless they react. The shorter line becomes crooked. A man forming the bridge yells.)

—They're shooting! Hold tight!

(The sound of a police whistle. Policemen arrive, dressed like the cops in Charlie Chaplin's *The Kid,* with large, prehistoric-type clubs. Music is heard. Their acting is crude. They immediately start hitting those in the longer line over the head. The sound of the clubs: Plac! Plac! Plac! Those hit fall into artificially distorted poses. The men rush the bridge of Martin Fisherman, crushing the captured player, who screams.)

GUIDE: Kids today! They don't know how to play peacefully! Let's get out of the way. I wonder if they'll tie them up. (warns a policeman) Not the audience! (The policeman moves his head like Harpo Marx. He spins around like an acrobat, beating on actors mixed in with the public, acting as audience members. Very confused.) On the double, ladies and gentlemen, quickly! Let's go! No stragglers! My group this way! Forward! Toward the music! (Music floats in the air, disappears.) Now what? (He opens his hands in a gesture of incomprehension. Taking advantage of the GUIDE's position, someone comes forward and puts a tin plate full of garbage in his hands. To this person, absolutely astonished.) What is this? (protests) Not to me you don't! This is not what I get paid for! Who do they think they are?

(Meanwhile, the game of Martin Fisherman has stopped. The policemen and actors from the shorter line carry off those who were knocked unconscious and throw them into a room.)

GUIDE: (to the group) With so much confusion, I forgot about the catacombs. You'll end up leaving without seeing anything.

WOMAN'S VOICE:

> "The water was black there
> under the branches.
> When it reached the bridge
> it stopped and sang."[13]

GUIDE: (pleased) Her again! What persistence! You want to risk it? Sooner or later it's got to improve!

(He opens the door. The people inside won't let him in.)

Scene 16

ACTOR #1: Sorry, old man. You can't come in. Off-limits.

GUIDE: Why not? I'm bringing people.

ACTOR #1: No, old man. We're rehearsing.

GUIDE: So what? Aren't you getting tired?

ACTOR #1: No! (He closes the door.)

GUIDE: (outraged) What balls. Sorry. (He remembers something, smiles.) They're not gonna fuck with me. Psss! This way! There's another entrance! (He leads them along a passageway. They pass a vertical box like the others, only bigger. Naturally.) Just a moment. (He opens the door of the box. Inside, two men are plastered together. The GUIDE puts the tin plate on their shoulders. They stretch their necks desperately, trying to suck up what's on the plate. It falls. Matter of factly, to the audience.) They let it fall! What idiots! (He closes the door.)

Scene 17

GUIDE: Don't make a sound. Walk on tiptoe. Don't say a word. (They enter a room. Folding screens around an illuminated central space.) Sssh . . . Silence . . . (The group watches the scene through the folding screens. Two actors and two actresses are rehearsing *Othello,* in rehearsal clothes. Actress #1, as Desdemona, is already dead on the floor.)

ACTOR #1: (as Iago)

Villainous whore![14]

ACTRESS #2: (as Emilia)

She give it Cassio? No, alas, I found it,
And I did give't my husband.

ACTOR #1:

Filth, thou liest!

GUIDE: Such language!

ACTRESS #2: (as Emilia)

By heaven, I do not, I do not, gentlemen.
O murd'rous coxcomb! What should such a fool
Do with so good a wife?

ACTOR #2: (as Othello)

Are there no stones in heaven
But what serves for the thunder?—Precious villain!

(Othello runs at Iago. Iago strikes Emilia and leaves. ACTOR #1 marks his exit and sits off to one side. A POLICEMAN enters in Isabellesque attire.)

POLICEMAN #1: (to ACTOR #2) You killed those two women! Villain! Viper!

(The ACTRESSES get up, go sit down. They watch calmly, a bit surprised.)

ACTOR #1: Who told this guy to come in?

POLICEMAN #1: (acting, calling his men) Over here, men. Here!

ACTOR #1: Go act for the other side. Who called you. Get out of here!

POLICEMAN #1: Thou hast no weapon, and perforce must suffer. They are dead.

ACTRESS #1: (joking) I am dead!

ACTRESS #2: (sings)

> Willow, willow, willow.
> Moor, she was chaste. She loved thee, cruel Moor!

ACTOR #1: Stop! (to the POLICEMAN) Will you beat it!

POLICEMAN #1: To raise your sword against a woman!

ACTOR #2: What are you talking about?

ACTOR #1: The guy's a mental case. Beat it! (He pushes him toward the door.) Out! (returns) Better keep the door locked. There's no telling who could walk in. Let's go, girls. That guy stank worse than a pig. (claps his hands) One more time!

POLICEMAN #1: (draws his sword) No, traitor!

ACTOR #2: (returns. In spite of himself, in character.) Wrench his sword from him.

POLICEMAN #1:

> Torments will ope your lips.

ACTOR #2:

> Well, thou dost best.

ACTOR #1: Cut! Right there!

POLICEMAN #1: Officers, come here! (Another POLICEMAN enters, dressed in the same style.)

POLICEMAN #2: What's happening, sir?

POLICEMAN #1: (He shows him the vial he's just taken from his own pocket.) Trotyl! And the women are dead! Oh my! O thou pernicious caitiff!

POLICEMAN #2: (with his sword, rounds up the ACTORS, who move into a corner) Move it, or I'll take a slice! (The ACTRESSES let out an inappropriate laugh.)

POLICEMAN #1: Take them, too, for having laughed at the wrong time! (in a dramatic voice)

> To you, Lord Governor,
> Remains the censure of this hellish villain,
> The time, the place, the torture, O, enforce it!
> Myself will straight aboard, and to the state
> This heavy act with heavy heart relate.

(He takes a gun from his pocket, forces the actors to exit.)

GUIDE: (to his group) A bit confusing, the way that happened, don't you think? So you understand. (He walks into the light. In a professional, dry and rapid voice.) Explanation: For Foreigners. (fierce and rude) Does anyone really need an explanation? If you want to act like actors, just go into a tenement and howl like dogs, throw a good scare into people. If you don't have money, people will be even more afraid. Why scream? Why pretend? When no one can open his mouth, why would anyone scream gratuitously? (He waits for a response, which he doesn't get.) Okay then! (resumes his professional tone) August 6, 1971. The police burst into an old house with many rooms, like this one, in the city of Santa Fe. In one of the rooms they find eight hundred grams of trotyl. They say. One journalist and three members of the Grupo 67 theater are arrested. They're taken to Buenos Aires on suspicion of subversive actions. The district attorney recommended they be absolved on the benefit of doubt. They were absolved May 24, 1972. (change of tone) Few are called, many are chosen. Nine months in the cage. In misery. Well, that's life! (He leaves the illuminated space, goes back to his group.) Wait! The show goes on!

Scene 18

A sort of deformed CHILD-MONSTER, dressed in a floor-length white shirt with lots of lace and frills. He is heavily made-up. Others disguised as CHILDREN follow. The CHILD-MONSTER clutches a club. They sing.)

CHILDREN:

> Anton, Anton Pirulero
> each one, each one
> attends to his game
> and he who does not
> he who does not
> will suffer the blame.

(The CHILDREN sit in a circle around the CHILD-MONSTER, who calls to one of the bigger children and gives him the club. The latter stays outside the ring. They play Anton Pirulero, in which the child playing Anton is in the center of the circle, turning around and around, his arms extended like wings. The others keep singing and pretend to play musical instruments— guitar, cornet, violin, etc. They have to be very alert, for if Anton Pirulero stops and points at one of them with his arm and that child isn't moving his own arms like Anton, then that child loses. He who loses three times is out. The game is played singing, and very fast.)

CHILD-MONSTER: (He is Anton Pirulero. In an out-of-tune sing-song.)

> Anton, Anton Pirulero
> each one, each one
> attends to his game
> and he who does not
> he who does not
> will suffer the blame.

(Now they play only guitar. The child with the club goes to the one who has changed places with Anton and hits him. The child falls. The game continues, faster every time. The CHILD-MONSTER never finishes his song, the game falls apart, and the child with the club hits out indiscriminately. Finally, the only ones left unharmed are the CHILD-MONSTER and the character with the club. They wave their arms and sing. The CHILD-MONSTER glares at the other one, more and more menacingly. He aims with his finger as though it were a revolver and kills the other child. Pum! He plays alone, his gestures increasingly spastic. The song "Anton Pirulero" becomes unintelligible. The lights go out.)

GUIDE: What now? Why did they kill the lights?

VOICES: (singing)

> Anton, Anton Pirulero
> each one
> each one
> attends to his game.

(Lights up. In the same space, THREE MEN and a YOUNG WOMAN. The CHILD-MONSTER laughs in his labored way, waves his arms, stutters.)

CHILD-MONSTER: D-d-d-ow-ow-n-n-n! S-s-s-i-i-i-t-t-t-d-d-d-ow-n-n-n-n!

(He aims his hand like a revolver. The men and woman don't seem to notice his presence. They sit of their own volition.)

FIRST MAN: What is your game?

SECOND MAN: Fear.

FIRST MAN: And yours?

THIRD MAN: Fear.

FIRST MAN: (to the YOUNG WOMAN) What is your game?

YOUNG WOMAN: Fear. (pause) And the question.

FIRST MAN: What question?

YOUNG WOMAN: Why fear? My name is Marina. I am twenty years old. I am Greek, a prisoner, and I have been tortured. (The CHILD-MONSTER stutters low, furiously. He keeps playing, getting all tangled up in his own movements.)

> Time is altered, the years to come are altered
> You know where you will find me
> I, fear, I, death
> I, the memory beyond reach
> I, the recollection of the tenderness of your hands
> I, the sadness of our broken life

I will defeat "it's not my concern" with my

                                                anguish

blast their alien sleep with fireworks,

                                   horrible and indecent

with countless shootings I will fall on the indifference

of those who pass by

until they begin to ask, to ask themselves

THREE MEN: (in an even tone)

Why fear?
Why torture?
Why deaths?

(Stuttering and autistic, the CHILD-MONSTER plays.)

THREE MEN:

Who set limits?
Who once said: this much thirst
this much water?

Who once said: this much air
this much fire?

Who once said: here the ken
of men and women
here the bounds?

Only hope has sharp knees.
They are bleeding.

(darkness)

(The poem spoken by the YOUNG WOMAN was written by
Marina. The poem spoken by the THREE MEN is Juan Gelman's.[15])

GUIDE: Now what? There they go again cutting the light without warning me! I understand less and less. We're the ones
who bear the brunt of this show. I shit on poetry! Watch
your wallets. And I left my flashlight. This way, this way.
It's so dark! Don't touch each other! Whose little ass is this?

(He laughs. Opens the door. The passageway is illuminated.)
Ah! Light, more light! What a phrase! Only a genius could
come up with that one, eh?

WOMAN'S VOICE:

> "Ay-y-y, for the big horse
> who didn't like water"[16]

GUIDE: Still at it! Now that's perseverance! (Baroque music is
heard. The GUIDE puts his ear to the door. Unsure.) Do we
go in here? I don't remember. Oh well, let's do it! Come
along, gentlemen! You're almost there!

Scene 19

They enter another room. Two GUARDS are dressing a group of
squalid-looking characters who are handcuffed to the wall,
heavily made-up, with false eyelashes and lots of rouge. Some
are half-undressed, wearing only jackets and underwear. Others
wear bras and costume jewelry. The GUARDS move around
busily. They bring chairs. Make the prisoners sit. They arrange
them artistically, crossing their legs, raising their arms as
though they were holding cigarettes between their fingers. The
prisoners stay in these poses. During the development of this
scene, one GUARD—seated apart—recites with a melancholy
air.)

GUARD:

> You, who come from the shores of the Tagus
> Every day sing of my death
> Only this do I ask
> > with my dying breath
> Every day sing of my death
> You, who come from the shores of the Tagus.[17]

(A signal is heard. A line of frightened men and women enter.
Some carry small packages in their hands, obviously clothing or
food. The GUARD watches them.)

GUARD: No one enters without being checked. (He turns his face away. Raises and lowers his index finger mechanically, while the people pass in front of him and go out. Recites rapidly.) With pants, no. With skirts, no. With stockings, no. With packages, no. With children, no. With faces, no. (A PRETTY GIRL passes. He looks at her. His finger stops. Very nicely.)

> Twenty little hard ones, twenty little hard ones
> all in a roll, all in a roll
> twenty little hard ones
> in your little asshole.[18]
> May I?

PRETTY GIRL: (stupidly) What?

GUARD: (wiggles his finger obscenely) May I?

PRETTY GIRL: No!

GUARD: (pulls himself up, undiscouraged) To arms! To arms against the little asshole! Right over here!

(A group of guards enters at a trot. They rush the PRETTY GIRL and fling themselves on her as though she were the ball in a game of baseball. They roll with her out of the room.)

GUARD: (moves off, uninterested. Starts again with a melancholy air.)

> You, who come from the shores of the Tagus . . .

LITTLE OLD LADY: (the last of the visitors. She brings a sandwich wrapped in a handkerchief.) I've come to see my little son. He misbehaved.

GUARD: (deflated) Ah . . . Why didn't you bring him up better, madam?

LITTLE OLD LADY: He was always my wayward one!

GUARD: A good beating is what they need. They don't learn unless they bleed.

LITTLE OLD LADY: At ten years old, he was looking up the girls' skirts.

GUARD: (dumbfounded) Filthy!

LITTLE OLD LADY: (plaintive) I cut his little whistle, but it did no good!

GUARD: It's late to repent. Show me what you've brought!

LITTLE OLD LADY: (unwraps her handkerchief) A sandwich.

GUARD: (lifts the top of the bread) Ah! Extra testicles. No, madam! Here they only lose them. And for us that's work! Confiscated! (He takes the sandwich.) Out!

LITTLE OLD LADY: I want to see my son! Just once! Be generous! You have a mother too!

GUARD: Yeah, but she's not an old whore like you.

LITTLE OLD LADY: Why are you insulting me?

GUARD: (with disgust) You're old! (in another tone) All right. Go see him. I'm doing this for my mother. Sentimentality will be the end of me! (gestures toward one of the seated prisoners) There he is.

LITTLE OLD LADY: (goes toward an OUTLANDISH-LOOKING PRIS-ONER and embraces him) Son! (She separates, looks at him.) No, this isn't him. (hugs another) Son! (looks) No, this one either.

OUTLANDISH-LOOKING PRISONER: (opening his arms) Da-da-da-da!

GUARD: Choose already. Take this one. What's the difference.

LITTLE OLD LADY: (leaning toward the prisoner. Timidly.) Juan?

OUTLANDISH-LOOKING PRISONER: Da!

LITTLE OLD LADY: Son!

OUTLANDISH-LOOKING PRISONER: Da!

GUIDE: (to the group) Pretty depressing, wouldn't you say?

GUARD: What about you all? Over here, young men!

GUIDE: (raises his hands) No! Out, quick! (the sound of music) We were going to go dancing. We got the wrong room. (very distressed) Let's go dancing! Dancing! Move it! Let's beat it! Let's go, gentlemen. Let's go! (They exit.)

GUIDE: Ouf! A narrow escape! (He listens. The music gets louder. It's happy, catchy.) That's it. Come. (He leads his group to a large space, where at this moment all the other groups converge.) Leave the space open, ladies and gentlemen! If you would be so kind as to stand against the wall. That's it. Thank you, everyone.

(On one side of the performing space is a semitranslucent folding screen, behind which can be seen a long table. In the center, a group of women, dressed like stereotypical prostitutes, execute the gestures conventionally attributed to them: they smoke, show their legs, swing their purses, put on makeup. A man roughly pushes in two more prostitutes. They look at him with a mixture of fear and outrage. The other women observe the new arrivals curiously, then one offers each of the new women a cigarette. The music suddenly stops. One of the prostitutes starts dancing, moving slowly, singing a blues number in a gravelly voice. A line of FOUR MEN enter at a trot, leading a prisoner with his eyes bandaged, to the center. They sing.)

FOUR MEN:

> We have come, we have come
> To have some fun!

(The PROSTITUTES watch them. The one dancing gradually slows down the rhythm until she is moving in place, singing inaudibly. The men spin the prisoner around until he becomes completely disoriented.)

MAN #1: Let's play the Little Blind Cock!

MAN #2: Cockadoodledoo!

(They play, rapidly poking and moving away from the prisoner, who searches for them with his arms outstretched.)

MAN #1: Play! Head down!

MAN #3: There are beams!

MAN #4: You could break your head open!

(They play, yell "Cockadoodledoo!" One of the PROSTITUTES comes forward. She first starts to join in the game, then stretches her hand toward the prisoner's bandage.)

MAN #1: (pushes her away) Get out of here! This is our game! In your place, whore!

MAN #2: (poking the prisoner) He's sweating! He's hot!

MEN #1, #3, and #4: (in a chorus) Make him strip! Make him strip!

(Maintaining an ambiguous air of play and violence, they take off his jacket, his pants, his shirt; they throw his clothes, which flutter around.)

MAN #1: Hard-boiled egg! Let's play hard-boiled egg!

(They fight like children.)

MAN #2: Me! Me!

MAN #3: Get out! Me!

(They play. The prisoner holds his body rigid while the others rush him, tie him up. Finally, one of the men hits him on the head. The prisoner falls.)

MAN #4: We warned you!

MAN #1: A beam, idiot!

MAN #2: We told you to keep your head down!

(They drag the prisoner behind the screen. Through the screen, one can see fuzzily that they are strapping him down on the table. A scream. Instantaneously, the volume of the music shoots up; two of the men come out from behind the screen.)

TWO MEN:

> Girls, if you want to sing,
> it's not prohibited!

(They clap. The PROSTITUTES don't move.)

Sing!

(The PROSTITUTES, forced into it, clap and sing. Again the music gets louder.)

>Girls, if you want to dance,
>it's not prohibited!

(The PROSTITUTES dance. Behind the screen, one can see the shadow of the two men moving away from the table. The hand of the prisoner falls softly. At the same time, the PROSTITUTES freeze in a musical comedy finale. The music stops. The lights go out, then come up again. The actors disperse, naturally. They take down the screen. The dead man gets up from the table, gathers his clothes, and begins to dress. Only the prisoners seated against the wall remain immobile.)

GUIDE: (drily) Ladies and gentlemen, what are you waiting for? The show is over. (House lights come up.)

GUIDE 2: (resentfully)

>If you clap enthusiastically in all good haste
>your hands won't go to waste!

(He claps, and the GUIDES and actors present imitate him.)

GUIDE:

>Theater imitates life
>If you don't clap
>It means that life is rotten to the core
>And we may as well just head for the door.

(He moves the audience out toward the door. From far away can be heard police sirens. Even when the audience is near the exit, they can hear.)

>Who once said: here the ken
>of men and women
>here the bounds?

(after a moment, repeat)

>Who once said: here the ken
>of men and women
>here the bounds?

>Curtain

Translator's Notes

1. "Carnation, sleep and dream," sung by a "sweet" female Voice, the Mother in scene 5, and other voices elsewhere, is from García Lorca's *Bodas de sangre,* or *Blood Wedding,* scene 2. I use the translation by James Graham-Luján and Richard L. O'Connell in *Three Tragedies of Federico García Lorca: Blood Wedding, Yerma, Bernarda Alba* (New York: New Directions, 1955). In the original, Gambaro used only "Nana, niño, nana, del caballo grande que no quiso el agua," repeated over and over. For the English version, I chose to use many more fragments of the lullabye over the course of the play. Gambaro approved this choice in her letter to me of March 28, 1986.

2. Stanley Milgram describes this experiment in his book *Obedience to Authority* (New York: Harper and Row, 1974). See Introduction, n. 10.

3. The Mother sings fragments from the *Blood Wedding* lullabye.

4. The disappearance of Nestor Martins and his client Nildo Zenteno was in fact one of the first. It happened during the term of de facto president General Levingston, who had come to power in a coup d'état, unseating the previous de facto president, General Onganía.

5. This Guide is different from the Guide in scene 6. Since the order of the scenes is up to the director, however, this Guide will be called Guide #2 only in scene 7, where the shift occurs.

6. General José de San Martín, the liberator (El Libertador) of the southern part of South America, is an Argentine national hero.

7. The Woman's Voice in this scene sings from the *Blood Wedding* lullabye.

8. RAF, or Revolutionary Armed Forces, is the translation of the name of FAR, Fuerza Armada Revolucionaria, a left-wing guerrilla group.

9. "Tell Grandma that the hem was turned here" is an encoded way of communicating the arrest.

10. Roberto Quieto, whose surname in fact means "quiet," was a prominent, highly respected liberal lawyer. Unbeknownst to most, he was also a powerful member of the Montoneros, the premier left-wing guerrilla organization.

11. The Boca Juniors are one of the most important Argentine soccer teams. Their home stadium is in the Buenos Aires neighborhood of La Boca, traditionally an Italian working-class section. San Lorenzo is another team from Greater Buenos Aires. Soccer is by far the most passionately followed sport in Argentina.

12. "Of our respect / Here's a token" is the couplet substituted for "violín, violón / es la mejor razón." See "Crisis, Terror, Disappearance."

13. The Woman's Voice sings lines from the *Blood Wedding* lullabye.

14. Lines from *Othello* are taken from act 5, scene 2, lines 229–35, 248–49, 256, 287, 306–7, 317, 367–71. All are found on pages 1239–40 of *The Riverside Shakespeare* (Boston: Houghton Mifflin, 1974).

15. Gelman's lines are: "Quien puso limites? / Quien dijo alguna vez: hasta aquí la sed? hasta aquí el agua? / Quien dijo alguna vez: hasta aquí

el aire, hasta aquí el fuego? / Quien dijo alguna vez: hasta aquí el
hombre, hasta aquí, no? / Solo la esperanza tiene las rodillas nitidas.
/ Sangran."

16. The Woman's Voice sings from the *Blood Wedding* lullabye.

17. "You, who come from the shores of the Tagus" is from a poem by
Garcilaso de la Vega. The Tagus River flows through western Spain and
Portugal. In her letter to me of March 28, 1986, Gambaro brought up
"substituting an English-language poem about death, provided of course
it's by a Master." I decided against this option since I felt that Gambaro's
appropriation of Garcilaso was important as a reference to a specific age,
place, and literary tradition. One of the greatest poets of the Spanish
Golden Age, Garcilaso influenced not only San Juan de la Cruz, Lope de
Vega, and Cervantes but also Rafael Alberti, Pedro Salinas, Miguel
Hernández, and other twentieth-century Spanish and Latin American
poets. The original reads: "Vosotros, los del Tajo en su ribera / Cantáreis
mi muerte cada dia / Este descanso llevaré aunque muera / Que cada día
cantáreis mi muerte, / Vosotros, los del Tajo en su ribera."

18. "Twenty little hard ones" is from García Lorca's *Los títeres de
cachiporra*. The original reads: "Veinte duritos y veinte duritos / y un
rollito de veinte duritos / en el agujero del culito."

Antígona Furiosa

To Laura Yusem and Bettina Muraña

Characters

Antígona

Coryphaeus

Antinous

This play premiered on September 24, 1986, at the Goethe Institute in Buenos Aires, with the following cast and artistic crew:

ANTIGONA	Bettina Muraña
CORYPHAEUS	Norberto Vieyra
ANTINOUS	Ivan Moschner
SET DESIGN	Graciela Galán, Juan Carlos Distéfano
COSTUMES	Graciela Galán
CREON'S SHELL	Juan Carlos Distéfano
ASSISTANT DIRECTOR	Jerry Brignone
DIRECTOR, MISE-EN-SCENE	Laura Yusem

Translator's Note

Creon is represented by a movable shell. When Coryphaeus puts on the shell, obviously he is assuming the power and the throne.

In Laura Yusem's production, Antígona's cell was represented by a pyramidal cage located in the center of the performance space. The play opened with Antígona hanged on one of the bars of this cage. Antígona never exited her cage.

The Chorus moved in the space outside the cage, set up with several café tables, each with two chairs. (One table would suffice.)

Creon's shell (torso, helmet, and arms) was made of painted polyester. It was used in a variety of ways: worn by the actor, held like a shield, or manipulated like a marionette. Toward the end of the play, it was abandoned in an old wheelbarrow.

The audience was seated all around the performance space.

Gambaro appropriates lines from Ophelia's song in *Hamlet,* act 4, scene 5, and from a Spanish translation of Sophocles's *Antigone.* Where Gambaro takes lines directly from her edition of Sophocles, I generally do the same, using Elizabeth Wyckoff's elegant English translation, published in David Grene and Richmond Lattimore, eds., *Sophocles I* (Chicago: University of Chicago Press, 1954). Where Gambaro paraphrases her edition of Sophocles, generally I do likewise.

ANTIGONA hanged. In her hair is a crown of withered white flowers. After a moment, she slowly loosens and removes the rope from around her neck, adjusts her dirty white dress. She sways, humming. Sitting together at a round table, two men dressed in street clothes are having coffee. CORYPHAEUS plays with a flexible little straw. He tears small pieces from his paper napkin and puts them together like flowers. He does so distractedly, with a mocking smile.

CORYPHAEUS: Who is that? Ophelia? (They laugh. ANTIGONA looks at them.) Waiter, another coffee!

ANTIGONA: (sings)

> "He is dead and gone, lady,
>   He is dead and gone,
> At his head a grass-green turf,
>   At his heels a stone."

CORYPHAEUS: There should be, but there isn't. You see grass? You see stone? You see a tomb?

ANTINOUS: Nothing!

ANTIGONA: (sings)

> "Larded with all sweet flowers;
> Which bewept to the grave did not go
>   With true-love showers."

(She looks curiously at the cups.) What are you drinking?

CORYPHAEUS: Coffee.

ANTIGONA: Coffee? What is that?

CORYPHAEUS: Try it.

ANTIGONA: No. (She points.) Dark as poison.

CORYPHAEUS: (instantly seizing on the word) Yes, we're poisoning ourselves! (He laughs.) I am dead! (He gets up, stiff, arms stretched out in front of him. Gasps hoarsely.)

137

ANTINOUS: No one touch him! Forbidden! His plague is contagious. He'll contaminate the city!

ANTIGONA: Forbidden! Forbidden? (As though dissociated from what she is doing, she removes Coryphaeus's crown and smashes it.)

ANTINOUS: She took your little crown!

CORYPHAEUS: No one will bury me!

ANTINOUS: No one.

CORYPHAEUS: The dogs will eat me. (gasps hoarsely)

ANTINOUS: Poor little guy! (He embraces CORYPHAEUS. They laugh, clap each other on the back.)

CORYPHAEUS: (offers ANTIGONA his chair) You want to sit down?

ANTIGONA: No. They're fighting now.

ANTINOUS: (kidding) Is that so?

CORYPHAEUS: Yes. They'll cut each other up with their swords. Fall down and go boom! And you'll be the nurse! (He approaches her with an ambiguous intention that ANTIGONA doesn't register; she just moves away.) How will you care for them? Where?

ANTIGONA: I will be the one who attempts it.

CORYPHAEUS: What?

ANTIGONA: To bury Polynices, my brother.

CORYPHAEUS: (mockingly) Forbidden! Forbidden! The king has forbidden it! *I* have forbidden it.

ANTINOUS: No one may touch him!

CORYPHAEUS: Who dares . . . (gestures, cutting his throat)

ANTIGONA: She didn't want to help me.

CORYPHAEUS: She? Who is she?

ANTIGONA: Ismene, my sister. I did it alone. No one helped me. Not even Haemon, my brave one, whom I will not wed.

CORYPHAEUS: And when is it to be, this shotgun wedding? (He

laughs, very amused; ANTINOUS joins in. They elbow each other and clap each other on the back.)

ANTIGONA: Whom I will *not* wed. For me there will be no wedding.

CORYPHAEUS: (benignly) What a pity. (jabs ANTINOUS to get his attention)

ANTINOUS: (hurriedly) A pity.

ANTIGONA: Nor wedding night.

CORYPHAEUS: Logical.

ANTINOUS: (like an echo) Logical.

ANTIGONA: Nor children. I will die . . . alone.

(The battle. An eruption of metallic clanging of swords, stamping of horses, screams and cries. ANTIGONA moves away. Watches from the palace. She falls to the ground, hitting her legs, rolling from one side to the other, in a rhythm that builds to a paroxysmic crescendo, as though she endures the suffering of battle in her own flesh.)

ANTIGONA: (screams) Eteocles, Polynices, my brothers, my brothers!

CORYPHAEUS: (approaching her) Such grieving can only come to grief. What is this crazy girl trying to do?

ANTINOUS: Bury Polynices is what she's trying to do—on such a beautiful morning!

CORYPHAEUS: They say that Eteocles and Polynices were to share the crown—one year one, one year the other. But power tastes sweet. Sticks like honey to the fly. Eteocles didn't want to share it.

ANTINOUS: Another might have relented. Not Polynices!

CORYPHAEUS: He attacked at the seven gates of the city and fell vanquished, at the seventh! (He laughs.) And then faced off with his brother Eteocles.

ANTIGONA: They died by each other's swords! Eteocles, Polynices! My brothers! My brothers!

CORYPHAEUS: (returns to the table) Always fights, battles, and blood. And the mad girl who should be hanged. Remembering the dead is like grinding water with a mortar and pestle—useless. Waiter, more coffee!

ANTINOUS: (timid) It didn't happen very long ago.

CORYPHAEUS: (ferocious) It happened. Now on to something else!

ANTINOUS: Why don't we celebrate?

CORYPHAEUS: (darkly) What is there to celebrate?

ANTINOUS: (He lights up. Stupidly.) That peace has returned!

CORYPHAEUS: (laughs) I'll drink to that! Let's have a toast! What'll it be?

ANTINOUS: Wine?

CORYPHAEUS: Yes, lots of wine! And no coffee! (mimics ANTIGONA) What is that dark liquid? Poison! (laughs, gasps hoarsely, faking a death rattle. After a moment, ANTINOUS joins in. ANTIGONA walks among her dead, in a strange gait in which she falls and recovers, falls and recovers.)

ANTIGONA: Corpses! Corpses! I walk on the dead. The dead surround me. Caress me . . . embrace me . . . Ask me . . . What?

CORYPHAEUS: (comes forward)

> Creon. Creon applies the law. Creon.
> Creon applies the law, in the matter of the traitor and
>   the true.
> Creon applies the law, touching on the dead
>   and the living.
> The same law.
> Creon will not permit burial for Polynices who wanted
>   to be consumed
> in blood and fire
> Blood and fire the land of his parents. His body will be
>   dinner
> dinner for the dogs and birds of prey. Creon Creon
> His law says:
> Eteocles will be honored

And Polynices
feast for the dogs. Feast and putrefaction.
Let no one come near—dare—to come near, like the
    mad girl
circling, circling the unburied unburied unburied corpse

(He returns to his place, sits down.)

No fool is fool as far as loving death. That will be the price.

ANTIGONA: My mother lay down with my father, who was born
of her belly, and thus we were begotten. And in this chain of
the living and the dead, I will pay for their wrongdoings.
And my own. There he is. Polynices. Polynices, my most be-
loved brother. For him, Creon will not allow burial, mourning, or tears. Only shame. A mouthful for the birds of prey.

CORYPHAEUS: Who challenges Creon will die.

ANTIGONA: Do you see me, Creon? I am crying! Do you hear
me, Creon? (deep lament, raw and guttural)

CORYPHAEUS: I heard nothing! I heard nothing! (He sings stam-
meringly, but with mocking undertone.) "There is no . . .
mourning be-be-be-neath the tra-tra-anquil sky!"

ANTINOUS: Forbidden! (He shakes CORYPHAEUS.) It's forbidden,
right?

ANTIGONA: For whom? For those who wag their tails like dogs!
Not for me! Do you see me, Creon? I will bury him, with
these arms, with these hands! Polynices!

(long, silent howl upon discovering Polynices's corpse, which is
represented by only a shroud. ANTIGONA throws herself on him,
with her own body covering him from head to toe.)

ANTIGONA: Oh, Polynices, brother. Brother. Brother. I will be
your breath. (She pants as though she would revive him.)
Your mouth, your legs, your feet. I will cover you. I will
cover you.

CORYPHAEUS: Forbidden!

ANTIGONA: Creon has forbidden it. Cre-on, de-cree-on, decree
you will kill me.

CORYPHAEUS: That will be the price.

ANTIGONA: Brother, brother. I will be your body, your coffin, your earth!

CORYPHAEUS: Creon's law forbids it!

ANTIGONA: Neither God nor justice made the law. (She laughs.) The living are the great sepulchre of the dead! This is what Creon does not know! Nor his law!

CORYPHAEUS: (softly) As though he could know.

ANTINOUS: (softly) What?

CORYPHAEUS: Except for Polynices, whose death he redoubles, Creon kills only the living.

ANTINOUS: The sepulchres are linked! (laughs) One to the other.

CORYPHAEUS: Wisely. In a chain.

ANTIGONA: Memory also makes a chain. Neither Creon nor his law knows this. Polynices, I will be sod and stone. Neither dogs nor birds of prey will touch you. (with a maternal gesture) I will wash your body, comb your hair. (She does.) I will weep, Polynices . . . I will weep . . . Bastards!

(Ceremoniously, she scratches the earth with her fingernails, throws dry dust on the corpse, stretches out on it. She gets up, claps two large stones together, rhythmically, their sound marking a funeral dance.)

CORYPHAEUS: She is giving him the funeral rites. Better not to see acts that shouldn't be performed.

(He and ANTINOUS leave the table.)

ANTINOUS: (watching) She didn't manage to bury him. The earth was too hard.

CORYPHAEUS: That's how the guards caught her. Who holds a loved one dearer than his country is despicable.

ANTINOUS: Exactly!

CORYPHAEUS: (softly) Child, how did you not think of this? (He takes up Creon's effigy.)

ANTINOUS: (bows, exaggeratedly and satirically) The king! The king!

CORYPHAEUS: I am the king. Mine the power and the throne.

ANTINOUS: He'll settle this affair for you. Antígona. (gestures for ANTIGONA to come forward)

CORYPHAEUS: Ah! Antígona, who mortifies, who moans, who suffers fear and trembling.

ANTIGONA: (serenely comes forward) Fear and trembling, fear and trembling, fear and trembling.

CORYPHAEUS: You did what I forbade.

ANTIGONA: I admit the deed and don't deny it.

ANTINOUS: (frightened) She won't deny it!

CORYPHAEUS: You transgressed the law.

ANTIGONA: Neither God nor justice decreed the law.

CORYPHAEUS: You dared defy me, defy me.

ANTIGONA: I dared.

CORYPHAEUS: Mad!

ANTIGONA: He is mad who accuses me of dementia.

CORYPHAEUS: Pride is worth nothing when it's a neighbor's slave.

ANTIGONA: (pointing to ANTINOUS, mockingly) Isn't that what he is, neighbor? And you?

ANTINOUS: (proud) No!

CORYPHAEUS: Yes!

ANTINOUS: I am so! (disconcerted) The slave's neighbor or the neighbor's slave?

CORYPHAEUS: (like ANTIGONA, laughs) This girl attacks me breaking the laws, and now she adds a second offense: boasting and laughing.

ANTIGONA: He didn't laugh at me.

CORYPHAEUS:

> She, not I, would be the man
> if I let her go unpunished.
> Neither she nor her sister
> will escape the most terrible death.

ANTIGONA: (turns pale) Ismene? Why Ismene?

ANTINOUS: Yes. Why Ismene?

CORYPHAEUS: (comes out from under Creon's robe, anxious to get back in character) Why?

ANTIGONA: She didn't want to help me. She was afraid.

CORYPHAEUS: How could she not be afraid? She's barely a child. So tender!

ANTIGONA: Before Creon, I too was afraid.

ANTINOUS: He's our king!

ANTIGONA: And I a princess! Though destined for disgrace.

ANTINOUS: Yes! Daughter of Oedipus and Jocasta. Princess.

CORYPHAEUS:

> She's sad
> Why does the princess feel bad?
> From her mouth like a violet
> We have nothing but sighs

ANTINOUS:

> No kisses, no prayers, no lies

CORYPHAEUS:

> If only she could have kept quiet
> At the corpse of her brother not tarried
> To Haemon she could have been married.

ANTIGONA: Before Creon, I was afraid. But he didn't know. My king, my sire, I am afraid! I am bowed down with this ignoble weight called fear. Don't punish me with death. Let me marry Haemon, your son, know the pleasures of marriage and motherhood. I want to see my children grow, to grow old slowly. I am afraid! (She cries out her name, summoning pride.) Antígona! (She gets up, straight, defiant.) I did it! I did it!

CORYPHAEUS: You're mad!

ANTIGONA: Creon is mad. He thinks death harbors only minor

hatreds. He thinks the law is law because it comes out of his mouth.

CORYPHAEUS: Who is stronger, rules. That is the law.

ANTINOUS: Women don't fight against men!

ANTIGONA: As a woman, I was born to share love, not hate.

ANTINOUS: At times you forget yourself.

CORYPHAEUS: We heard you! And it's got a nice ring, ". . . born to share love, not hate"!

ANTIGONA: I said it to Creon, who always comes carrying his hate. Hate never comes alone.

CORYPHAEUS: Wrath. Injustice.

ANTIGONA: I rule.

CORYPHAEUS: No woman will rule me.

ANTIGONA: But you were ruled, humbled. Brought down by your own omnipotence.

ANTINOUS: I wouldn't say brought down.

CORYPHAEUS: (cruelly imitates him) I wouldn't say, I wouldn't say! Neither would I. Ismene was wiser.

ANTIGONA: She didn't want to help me. She was afraid. And with the fear of one who is guilty, she went before Creon. Polynices cries out for earth. Earth is what the dead ones ask for, not water or contempt. (groans like Ismene) Don't cry, Ismene. You don't want to help me. "Ssssh! Silence, let no one learn of your plan. Who touches Polynices's corpse will be stoned. I ask the dead to pardon me. I shall be obedient." To whom, Ismene? To Creon, the hangman?

CORYPHAEUS: Hangman. She said "hangman."

CORYPHAEUS and ANTINOUS:

> Power will not be outdone
> When it is questioned
> Blood begins to run.

(They lift the table and carry it to the other side of the space.)

ANTIGONA: I didn't want to make her do anything. I wanted to hold her, comfort her as when we were children, when she would come to me, crying, because they'd stolen her skipping stones or she'd hurt herself on the stairs. There, there, little one, my little one. But I heard myself shout. Rage! Rage! Coward, I hate you! May the whole world know that I will bury Polynices. Unconcealed, I will bury my dead one!

CORYPHAEUS: Stupidly, Ismene went to the palace—an innocent with the air of one who is guilty—knowing, when she most wanted to be ignorant.

ANTIGONA: (beating her breast) "I know! I know everything!" Before Creon, courage came to her, better courage than mine, for it was born of fear. "I was complicit, complicit." (She laughs, mocking.) She, complicit, whose love is only words!

CORYPHAEUS: I will not accept complicity that was not yours.

ANTINOUS: So you refused her?

CORYPHAEUS: Yes. Ismene, in disgrace, wanted to sail beside her into suffering. What would another girl—not Antígona—have done? Overflowing with gratitude, she would have opened her arms!

ANTIGONA: I closed them.

ANTINOUS: Insatiable! Unsatisfied!

CORYPHAEUS: Hers is the vice of pride. Pride plus heroism, where does it lead? ("cuts" his throat)

ANTIGONA: (sweetly) Ismene, dear face, sister, my little girl, I need the hardness of my own decision. Without envy, I want you to escape the death that awaits me. Creon called the two of us mad because we both defied him, we both scorned his laws. We wanted justice, I through justice itself and she through love.

CORYPHAEUS: You can talk as much as you like, but your fate is sealed.

ANTINOUS: (gets up and moves away) I don't want to see it. I've already seen too much!

CORYPHAEUS: (brings him back) Sit down. Haemon will come to plead for her.

ANTINOUS: I can see it all now. His face, full of grief . . .

CORYPHAEUS: Well, of course! Add two and two: Antígona's sentence plus the loss of his marriage . . .

ANTINOUS: Poor little guy!

CORYPHAEUS: He'll make use of a masterly saying.

ANTINOUS: Which one?

CORYPHAEUS: One can rule a desert beautifully alone.

ANTIGONA: Haemon, Haemon!

CORYPHAEUS: (goes toward Creon's effigy) He loves Antígona.

ANTINOUS: Don't take her away from him.

CORYPHAEUS: (in the effigy) I am not I. This is death. (He laughs low.) Haemon? (ANTIGONA turns toward him.) You're not furious?

ANTIGONA: (All her replies are in a neutral tone.) No.

CORYPHAEUS: I will be inflexible.

ANTIGONA: I know.

CORYPHAEUS: Nothing will modify my decision.

ANTIGONA: I will not try to change it.

CORYPHAEUS: I am glad. One wants submissive children, who will meet our enemies blow for blow and honor our friends.

ANTIGONA: It is just.

CORYPHAEUS: Anarchy is the worst blow. Who transgresses the law and tries to give me orders will never receive my praises. I trust only those who are obedient.

ANTIGONA: I would not dare to say your words are unreasonable. But others too may speak good sense. Your gaze intimidates. I can hear what the people are saying. Doesn't she merit praise and not punishment?

CORYPHAEUS: That woman has gone to your head.

ANTIGONA: I speak from the head, and not the heart.

CORYPHAEUS: In the voice of a woman. There are no colder arms than those of a perverse, indomitable woman.

ANTIGONA: Perverse? Indomitable.

CORYPHAEUS: Like that one. Spit in her face. Let her look for a husband in hell.

ANTIGONA: I will spit at her. (silence. She raises her hand to her face.) He didn't spit at me, Creon.

CORYPHAEUS: (comes out from behind the robe and faces ANTIGONA) You should be proud.

ANTIGONA: Of what?

CORYPHAEUS: That a youngster like Haemon is giving lessons to his father, the king!

ANTIGONA: If I am young, heed my actions rather than my age. Of Haemon's pride, I am proud.

CORYPHAEUS: (moves away toward the table, outraged) Youth!

ANTINOUS: Now it's all smoothed over, but what an argument! You could hear it as far as the corner.

CORYPHAEUS: If Haemon raised his voice, it was justified.

ANTINOUS: You said, "Youth!"

CORYPHAEUS: So what? I wasn't referring to Haemon. He spoke for us. He said what all of us were thinking.

ANTINOUS: (confused) What? (scratches his head)

CORYPHAEUS: "You condemned her unjustly."

ANTINOUS: Oh!

CORYPHAEUS: What lawyers did she have? What judges? Who was at her side?

ANTINOUS: Her father?

CORYPHAEUS: She has no father!

ANTINOUS: Her mother? (quick gestures of negation by CORYPHAEUS) Her brothers? (further gestures) Her friends? He got hold of her and decided: This one I am going to crush.

CORYPHAEUS: And we say: This girl here condemned? She protested that her brother, fallen in combat, would be deprived of a grave. Doesn't this merit praise and not punishment?

ANTINOUS: (pleased) That's what we said!

CORYPHAEUS: Responding to what we said, Creon . . . (makes a vulgar gesture)

ANTIGONA: Public outcry is always born of secret words. Who believes that he alone thinks or speaks like no one else is totally empty inside.

ANTINOUS: Haemon spoke very well!

CORYPHAEUS: So did Creon! He said, "I trust only those who are obedient. They will not violate the law."

ANTINOUS: (very confused) Only one should speak well so we won't be so confused!

CORYPHAEUS: Confusion I can easily resolve. (Majestically, he advances toward Creon's effigy, but he stops halfway. He turns toward ANTIGONA.) The city belongs to him who rules.

ANTIGONA: One can rule a desert beautifully alone.

CORYPHAEUS: There it is. The masterly saying.

ANTINOUS: (very confused) Here we go again. Who is right?

CORYPHAEUS: Then they insulted each other. Creon called his son stupid, and Haemon said his father spoke like a beardless youth!

ANTINOUS: His father?

CORYPHAEUS: His father! "You shall not marry her while she's alive," said Creon.

ANTINOUS: Good!

CORYPHAEUS: "Then she will die, but she won't die alone," answered Haemon.

ANTINOUS: What audacity!

CORYPHAEUS: What? To refute foolish words!

ANTINOUS: They weren't foolish!

CORYPHAEUS: (looks at him menacingly. Suddenly smiles.) Maybe . . . my weakness is that I am easily moved.

ANTIGONA: Creon sent for me—the hated runt—so that I would die in Haemon's presence and before his eyes.

CORYPHAEUS: It didn't happen. Haemon didn't want it.

ANTIGONA: I know he didn't want it.

CORYPHAEUS: "She will not die in my presence," said Haemon, "and you will never again lay eyes on me!" (He rises.) "Your obliging friends will let you abandon yourself to your furies. But you will never again lay eyes on me!"

ANTINOUS: Sit down! Don't leave me alone!

CORYPHAEUS: Why? What are you afraid of?

ANTINOUS: Nothing. (confidentially) I dared tell Creon that Haemon was feeling desperate. A serious thing at his age.

CORYPHAEUS: And what is that worth? What did you risk? I, I pleaded for Ismene! What was her crime? To have listened to the mad girl. She didn't touch the corpse.

ANTINOUS: Creon's no fool.

CORYPHAEUS: He pardoned her.

ANTINOUS: Yes, and then?

CORYPHAEUS: And then, what?

ANTINOUS: You settled it. "What death for Antígona?" you very nicely asked.

CORYPHAEUS: It was already decided. What could change it? I hid her in a hollow cave with food to last one day.

ANTIGONA: I made my last journey.

CORYPHAEUS: There, she will entreat death, beg that it not touch her.

ANTIGONA: Do not touch me! Oh, death, please do not touch me.

CORYPHAEUS: She will realize, a little late, that it's useless to petition death for life.

ANTIGONA: Nevertheless, I plead.

CORYPHAEUS: (sadly) Useless, but gratis!

ANTIGONA: I pleaded for sunlight. My eyes, not sated with the light.

CORYPHAEUS: Love, love! What a disaster! I mean for Haemon. But if desire wins out, where does that leave the laws of the land?

ANTINOUS: Yes, yes, but what do the laws have to do with Antígona? I watch her and . . .

CORYPHAEUS: She is going toward the bed in which all of us must lie.

ANTIGONA: I made my last journey. To say, "the last time." (Her voice becomes distorted.) La-ast time. To know . . . that further on there is no light, not a single voice. Death, that sleeps in everything that breathes, pulls me to its borders. I did not know the wedding night, or marriage hymn. I go a virgin. My marriage will be with death.

CORYPHAEUS: You're forgetting the advantages: you walk through the shadows in glory, exalted.

ANTINOUS: All the world approves of you!

CORYPHAEUS: No illnesses, no sufferings!

ANTINOUS: No sickliness from old age!

CORYPHAEUS: Of all of us, one might say, only you will descend unto death of your own volition. It's not so tragic.

ANTIGONA: Like Niobe, fate will put me to sleep under a mantle of stone.

CORYPHAEUS: But Niobe was a goddess born of gods. We are mortals, born of mortals.

ANTINOUS: Grandiose for her to say she shares the fate of gods! (He and CORYPHAEUS laugh.)

ANTIGONA: You're laughing at me!

CORYPHAEUS: No, no! (They laugh.)

ANTIGONA: Why offend me before my death, while I still breathe?

CORYPHAEUS: Look, it was a joke! Don't take offense!

(Chastised, they squeeze their lips together, swallowing their laughter.)

ANTIGONA: Oh, fortunate citizens, bear witness that no one wept with me . . .

CORYPHAEUS: My God, she's starting to pity herself! (They try to flee.)

ANTIGONA: Let the laws, these vile laws! drag me to a cave that will be my tomb. No one will hear my weeping; no one will be aware of my suffering. They will live in the light as though nothing were happening. With whom will I share my house? I will be separated from both humans and those who died, uncounted among the living and among the dead. I will disappear from the world, alive.

CORYPHAEUS: (kindly) Punishment always presupposes crime, my girl. There are no innocents.

ANTINOUS: (low) Never? (regains his composure) I approve— very well said!

CORYPHAEUS: And if punishment comes down on you, you did something you shouldn't have done. What do you expect? You brought your violence to its summit, and then you fell, violently.

ANTINOUS: Splat!

ANTIGONA: Ay, what an ill-fated wedding you arranged for me, brother! With your death your killed me, though I survived you.

ANTINOUS: This is breaking my heart!

CORYPHAEUS: Mine too. But for him who has it, power is invio-lable. How could she even think of opposing it? Don't whine, my girl. A destiny so within and so without the norm can't be paid in copper coins.

ANTINOUS: Her character did her in.

CORYPHAEUS: You should have listened to counsel. *Our* counsel!

ANTIGONA: The sun! The sun!

CORYPHAEUS: There it is. Look at it for the last time.

ANTIGONA: For the last time. They take me away without weeping, without friends, without a husband. At my death, neither tears nor lamentation. Only my own.

CORYPHAEUS: Did you look at the sun? Did you have a good taste? Did it warm you? Good, enough! If they let us mourn before our deaths, we would never die!

ANTINOUS: Enough! She won't quit!

CORYPHAEUS: I'll make her quit! (He goes toward Creon's effigy, stops midway.) These delays will be regretted! (wearing the robe) Lock her up! Leave her in that tomb. If she wishes to die there, let her die. If she wishes to live hidden under this roof, let her live. We will be cleared of her death, and she will have no contact with the living.

ANTINOUS: What wisdom! What is, is not; we kill and do not kill her.

ANTIGONA: Oh, tomb; oh, wedding chamber! House hollowed out of rock, eternal prison where I will be together with my own. As the term of my life expires, I am the last and most miserable to descend. But there at least my hope is great: when I arrive I will have my father's love, and your love too, mother, and yours, my brother. When they died, with my own hands I washed their bodies, performed the funeral rites. And now, for you, dear Polynices, I receive this sad reward. If I could have been a mother, I never would have done this for my children. Never for my dead husband would I have attempted such hardship. Polynices, Polynices, you know why I say so! I could have met another husband, conceived other children, in spite of my pain. But mother and father dead, no brother can ever be born. You will never again be born, Polynices. Creon has judged me, my brother.

CORYPHAEUS: (coming out of the robe) And well judged!

ANTIGONA: What law have I broken? What god offended? But how can I still believe in God? On whom may I call if my piety has earned me impious treatment? But if my persecutors are in the wrong, I want the same harm for them that they unjustly do to me! The same harm—no more, no less— the same harm!

ANTINOUS: Such a bigmouth.

CORYPHAEUS: Rancorous, for her to keep blowing up the same old wind! (with reserve, to ANTIGONA) There is something called repentance! It's not good for much, but it's comforting.

ANTINOUS: If we know already that she dies, why doesn't she die?

CORYPHAEUS: Creon said that we would regret letting her go so slowly. (low sound of wingbeats and cawing)

ANTIGONA: They're taking me away. See to what torture and by what judges I am condemned!

ANTINOUS: She is suffering.

CORYPHAEUS: One always suffers when celestial light is exchanged for the darkness of a prison. Many women have known a similar fate. When power is affronted and limits transgressed, my girl, payment is always in the currency of blood. (The sound of hoarse, sinister cawing grows louder. The sound of wingbeats rises and falls.) What is that noise?

ANTINOUS: Birds in spring.

CORYPHAEUS: (coldly) Stupid.

ANTINOUS: They insult me. I leave.

CORYPHAEUS: Stay! Something will happen at the last minute.

ANTIGONA: I didn't know. I didn't know that Creon . . .

ANTINOUS: Is someone going to defend her?

CORYPHAEUS: No, never!

ANTINOUS: So now what?

ANTIGONA: (pushes away enormous wings) Away! Away! (wails in terror, trying to protect herself. With effort, she regains her self-control.) No! Go ahead! Cover me with your stinking wings, peck at me with your beaks! (She offers herself, ferocious, her teeth clenched.) Bite! Bite! Don't pity me any more than Creon does . . .

ANTINOUS: I want to go home. I'm cold.

CORYPHAEUS: We're going already. I'd like another coffee. (rises with his cup in hand, looking for coffee. Stops in front of Creon's effigy.)

ANTINOUS: (Something falls on the table. He picks it up, full of disgust.) What is this? What is this *filth?*

CORYPHAEUS: Don't worry about it! Tiresias will come, and though blind, Tiresias the priest will settle everything. (He puts on Creon's robe.) What's new, old Tiresias? Your face—darkened as though doubly blind—frightens me. I never deviated from your counsel. Which is why I ruled this city well. (emphasizes) With skillful covenants. (pause) What is this filth? It's falling on *me!* (leaves, picking off the filth falling on him)

ANTINOUS: (hides with his hand something that fell on his arm, fearful and unmoving. Slowly moves his hand, while looking upward.) Plague!

CORYPHAEUS: What? Plague!

ANTINOUS: I want to go home!

CORYPHAEUS: The hungry birds are tearing Polynices's corpse to pieces. That's why they're screaming. They've eaten the flesh and blood of a dead man in the fray.

ANTINOUS: Let Tiresias settle this! I want to go home!

CORYPHAEUS: The plague will follow you home!

ANTINOUS: I'll lock myself in!

CORYPHAEUS: The plague will follow you! No God will hear our supplications. Damned birds!

ANTIGONA: A wrong permitted contaminates everyone. Hiding in our houses, devoured by fear, the plague will follow us.

CORYPHAEUS: Maybe not, if Tiresias obtains from Creon that which he stubbornly denied to you.

ANTIGONA: You won't convince Creon, Tiresias. Creon told you that the entire race of priests was money-mad. (She laughs.) And you replied that tyrants all grab at shameful gain. You got along well! (She pushes away the wings, whose flapping has decreased.) I am not afraid. What does Tiresias tell you? That you'll pay with the death of one born of your own blood . . . (It grows darker.) Hae . . . Haemon . . . for having thrown me in the grave and for keeping Polynices's corpse unburied. In Tiresias's mouth, truth and lies are mixed.

Don't be angry with a corpse. What victory can there be in killing someone who is dead?

CORYPHAEUS: Yes, that's what he will say.

ANTIGONA: Dogs, wolves, and vultures will tear my brother's body and with his remains befoul the altars.

CORYPHAEUS: Plague!

ANTIGONA: The cities are growing agitated.

CORYPHAEUS: Plague!

ANTIGONA: Tiresias, this frightens you! Easy to be a friend to power at its peak and then to separate when it declines. You pleaded for me, for Polynices torn apart. And out of fear, Creon pardoned me. (pause) I didn't know it. (The cawing and wingbeats cease.)

CORYPHAEUS: "I am afraid I will have to heed the laws," said Creon.

ANTINOUS: A little late for that.

CORYPHAEUS: He will also have to heed his feelings when Haemon . . . (gestures, stabbing himself)

ANTIGONA: (humming, puts on the crown of flowers) And so I married. (twists her neck and body in a strange manner, as though she is hanging, hanged) Death: bride, mother, sister . . .

CORYPHAEUS: Ah, the fury of Haemon!

ANTIGONA: Fury of youth!

CORYPHAEUS: Creon called to him, sobbing. How could you enter that tomb? I hear your voice, or do my senses deceive me? Move the stones that block the entrance. Haemon! I beg you! Come out from that tomb! (parodic sobbing)

ANTIGONA: Haemon wrapped his arms around my waist.

CORYPHAEUS: Then what did Haemon do? He spit on his father! (spits in ANTINOUS's face)

ANTINOUS: Not on me!

CORYPHAEUS: And drew his sword and . . . (attacks)

ANTINOUS: (jumping) Creon barely escaped.

CORYPHAEUS: It would have been better if he'd been killed. Is there anything worse than one's own misfortune? Not only Haemon, but also Eurydice, his mother, stabbed herself to death.

ANTINOUS: She too! No one's left!

CORYPHAEUS: Creon's left. (He puts on the robe.)

ANTIGONA: He sobbed, his arms around my waist.

CORYPHAEUS: Haemon, oh, wretch! In what misfortune do you wish to lose yourself?

ANTIGONA: His blow to Creon missed, and he threw himself upon his sword. Still breathing, he wrapped himself in my arms and died gasping . . . waves of blood . . . waves of blood . . . on my face . . . (suddenly screams) Haemon, Haemon, no! Don't die! Don't double my solitude.

ANTINOUS: All these problems from a lack of common sense! Right?

CORYPHAEUS: Ay, these minds and their mistakes! People of my lineage killing and being killed. Ay, son, son! All the calamity sowed in my family and on this earth! And now me, guilty! Against me, all the darts! I will suffer in this prison, on bread and water. (sobs sincerely)

ANTINOUS: (disconcerted) Prison, but you're still in power. What do you mean by prison? Bread and water, delicacies and wine? Bowing and scraping and ceremonies?

CORYPHAEUS: I will suffer until they understand!

ANTINOUS: You have a big heart that easily pardons . . .

ANTIGONA: His own crimes.

CORYPHAEUS: Mine were the power and the throne. (ashamed) Even now . . .

ANTINOUS: In spite of your terrible pain you enjoy yourself. Perfect happiness! Like us! (ANTIGONA lets out an animal cry.)

CORYPHAEUS: I pardon them! They know not what they are doing. I am the one to be condemned, I, who made a holocaust on my son, on my wife. Antígona, who brought so much harm down on my head and heritage, I pardon you!

ANTINOUS: (theatrical) Bravo! (CORYPHAEUS removes the robe, bows.)

ANTIGONA: (sings)

> "They bore him barefaced on the bier
> And in his grave rained many a tear."

I weep for you, Haemon! Blood, you had so much blood! (touches her face) Without and within, I am full of your blood. I don't want it . . . I don't want it. It's yours. Drink of your blood, Haemon. Recover your blood. Live!

ANTINOUS: Will he?

CORYPHAEUS: (smiling at his stupidity) A little difficult.

ANTINOUS: But . . .

CORYPHAEUS: (cuttingly) When there's blood involved, acts can't be mended, idiot!

ANTIGONA: (softly) You doubled my solitude. Why did you prefer nothingness to pain? Flight to the obstinacy of the conquered?

ANTINOUS: He was very young!

CORYPHAEUS: And you, why were you in such a hurry? (gestures, hanging himself)

ANTIGONA: I was afraid of hunger and thirst. Afraid I would weaken ignobly. At the last moment, crawl and beg.

ANTINOUS: The hardest hearts can soften "at the last moment." Didn't you hear him weeping? He pardoned you.

ANTIGONA: No. I still want to bury Polynices. I will *always* want to bury Polynices. Though I a thousand times will live, and he a thousand times will die.

ANTINOUS: Then Creon will *always* punish you.

CORYPHAEUS: And you a thousand times will die. You don't have to call death, my girl. She comes on her own. (smiles) Pressuring her is fatal.

ANTIGONA: Will there never be an end to this mockery?
Brother, I cannot endure these walls I cannot see, this air
that seals me in like stone. Thirst. (She touches the earthen
bowl, lifts it and brings it to her lips. Freezes.) I will drink
and stay thirsty, my lips will grow slack, my tongue will
grow thick like that of a mute animal. No. I refuse this bowl
of mercy that masks their cruelty. (Slowly, she turns it upside
down.) Mouth moist with my own saliva, I will go to my
death. Proudly, Haemon, I will go to my death. And you will
come running and lean on your sword. I didn't know. I was
born to share love, not hate. (long pause) But hate rules.
(furious) The rest is silence! (She kills herself, with fury.)

Curtain

Violent Displays

Griselda Gambaro and Argentina's Drama of Disappearance

> First we will kill all the subversives; then we will kill their collaborators; then . . . their sympathizers, then . . . those who remain indifferent; and finally we will kill the timid.
>
> —*General Iberico Saint Jean, governor of Buenos Aires, May 1976*

Griselda Gambaro is one of the most important and innovative playwrights in the world today. Not only is she singularly perceptive about the criminal machinations of the authoritarian governments she has lived under in Argentina from the 1960s to the present, but she is also keenly aware of the role of representation (social and theatrical) in maintaining or dismantling the political structure. Theater, as one system of representation, both reflects and constitutes society, a wider system of representation. Throughout her dramatic production from 1963 to the late 1980s, Gambaro's own violent brand of theater has exposed the theatricality of Argentina's political violence. Her first plays from the 1960s already foreshadow the abductions, "disappearances," and concentration camps, signaling the direction that Argentina's internal conflicts would take, culminating in the military coup and the infamous Dirty War (1976–83). Moreover, Gambaro is one of the very few Latin American playwrights who look at gender as a socially overdetermined representation and who call our attention to how easily violence in the political "body" is directed at the female body both literally and metaphorically.

The political use of public spectacle to control the population's attention was perhaps best exploited in Argentina's recent history by Juan Perón (president, 1946–55, 1973–74)—the massive rallies, slogans, posters, propaganda of national unity under El Líder (the Leader), the mythification of Evita as the Lady of Hope and Standard-Bearer of the Poor, and Perón's monumental staging of national mourning and solidarity upon her death. All of these served to cover Argentina's growing economic and political crisis. The competing displays of power, however, became increasingly evident after Juan Carlos Onganía's exceptionally repressive coup and his "ostentatious parade of its power" in 1966, which was opposed by riots and strikes staged by students and workers in Córdoba. For two days in 1969 Córdoba turned into "a theatre for pitched battles between rioters and police."[1] The prevalent political violence of the 1960s developed into the orchestrated state terrorism of the 1970s. During the last of Argentina's numerous dictatorships (1976–83), the military junta waged its Dirty War against its civilian population. The military men also relied heavily on spectacle to signal and consolidate power. They were aggressively visible, on parade, in uniform, wielding their weapons for all the world to see. The tactics they employed to disrupt and paralyze the population were also highly dramatic. Men and women were abducted in broad daylight; they "disappeared" as if by magic. As in Elizabethan drama, corpses reappeared out of nowhere at strategic moments. The theatricality of terrorism endowed the national frame with a strange spectacularity. A tragic aura enveloped the country; the tension mounted; the atomized population was frozen in suspense. The weekly march of the Mothers of the Plaza de Mayo was a physical reminder of those who had simply disappeared off the face of the earth.

Gambaro's theater over the past three decades has captured the constants associated with sociopolitical crisis as well as the changes in perspective that lead to an understanding of what crisis means and whose interests it serves. The perspective from which her characters view the crisis develops from the passive acceptance of catastrophe in the 1960s to the acute awareness in the 1980s that their passivity has contributed to their own annihilation. This awareness permits the characters to oppose those in power and fight back. Unlike those in most Latin American drama, Gambaro's characters who start to fight back against authority in the 1980s are women. As her work progresses, the tone of Gambaro's questioning becomes more urgent, and her theatrical formulation becomes more pointed, disruptive, and direct. Although many of the themes, constructions, and technical devices remain recognizable throughout Gambaro's dramaturgy, it is possible to divide her work into three stages.

Gambaro's plays from the 1960s, as I discuss at length in my recent book, are a theater of crisis.[2] The victims find themselves suddenly placed in a world that they cannot recognize or understand. Although they find their lives threatened for no apparent reason, their victimizers assure them that nothing unusual is happening; everything is normal. The victims grasp at this reassurance and refuse to see their predicament even as they face death. During the early 1970s, Gambaro's theater becomes a drama of disappearance obsessed with the "missing." And not just people are missing. Everything that has previously made sense— from life-sustaining values to reason itself—has disappeared. During the 1980s, Gambaro's plays reveal a critical awareness of the causes and effects of sociopolitical crisis and the very real benefits of permanent crisis to military leaders who needed to destabilize their population in order to maintain power. These plays continue to portray the victimizer-victim relationship that dominates Gambaro's work, but now the victims refuse to deceive themselves and will no longer play along passively in the drama of their own annihilation.

Gambaro's early plays, *The Walls (Las paredes,* 1963), *The Blunder (El desatino,* 1965), *The Siamese Twins (Los siameses,* 1965), and *The Camp (El campo,* 1967), dramatize the progressive decomposition of social and judicial structures designed to keep violence contained and thus under control. *The Blunder* and *Siamese Twins* demonstrate that violence within family circles is inextricable from rampant social violence. They feed each other and transform all relationships, even the closest ones, into that of victimizer-victim. *The Camp* depicts a neo-Nazi concentration camp of the kind that was in fact to appear in Argentina a decade later; there is evidence of some 340 such camps operating during the Dirty War. *The Camp,* one of Gambaro's finest plays, portrays a world of complete ambiguity that disorients outsiders. Martin, who stumbles into the place thinking he has a legitimate job as an accountant at a "school," is misled by the highly theatrical and artificial sounds, explanations, and costumes that have been devised to put him (and all other observers) off guard. This play is also interesting in that it presents gender as a socially overdetermined construct. Emma, an emaciated, flea-ridden victim in the camp, is forced to pretend that she is an elegant woman, an artist, a star. She is made to wear a grotesque blond wig over her shaved head and a dirty dish towel as a "train" pinned onto her prisoner's gown. Now, as this supposedly glamorous figure, she is made to mince seductively onstage and perform for the male prisoners, who of course are encouraged to jeer at her and utter sexist remarks. Everyone suffers during repressive regimes, Gambaro tells us, but women are abused and humiliated because they are women, in addition to all the other politically "necessary" reasons. Not only are they systematically raped, but they are also humiliated for assuming the sexual identity that has been foisted on them.

Throughout these plays contradictions and confusion multiply. The known universe becomes unknowable. The familiar becomes strange and threatening as the world melts into a terrifying void whose parameters recede and contract. The recurring images in these plays include the collapse of boundaries separating inner from outer, private from public, self from other. The seemingly private room in *The Walls* becomes a prison cell. The walls physically move in to crush the Young Man. Nor is the Young Man's identity perceived as stable or individuated. He is abducted because someone mistakes him for Ruperto de Hentzau or Hentcau, the fictitious villain of *The Prisoner of Zenda*. The causes of the collapse, both physical and metaphoric, remain unexamined and unexplained.

Gambaro's characters of this period respond to crisis in two distinguishable ways. The victimizers create or manipulate the crisis. As Gambaro makes emphatically clear here, victimizers and torturers are made, not born. In some plays, *The Walls* for example, the victimizers, like theater directors, set the drama in motion. Those victimizers who do not personally devise the catastrophic situation readily adapt to it. Both kinds of victimizers are highly theatrical: the former because they have to deceive potential victims and onlookers and control their perceptions; the latter because in adapting to atrocity they have to repress or "split off" a part of their personalities. They become either one-dimensional, like traditional stock characters in drama, or split into two, of which the victims (and we as audience) see only one part. The victims, on the other hand, are incapacitated by crisis. They cannot orient themselves. Their immediate response is to deny the extent or even the existence of danger. This denial, consequently, allows for the displacement of responsibility. Because the Young Man has done nothing *wrong,* he assumes that things will eventually be put *right*—by someone else. All he has to do is wait. Innocence "normally" guarantees freedom. After all, he comforts himself, "we're not in a country full of madmen." The cell-room set, however, functions as a transformer of norms. Nothing comes out "normal." The very concept of normality dies in that room. Soon he cannot trust his own senses; the lights go on and off, undermining all notions of night and day. He hears screams from the next room, but the Usher convinces him not to trust his own ears. The Young Man, faced with the chaotic situation, renounces his own critical capacity to assess and address the situation.

One of the characteristics of Gambaro's early plays is that her victims star in dramas of persecution that they fail to recognize as their own. They make up explanations that seem to be borrowed from other scripts, given that they are flagrantly out of keeping with the reality we see with our own eyes. Unable to fathom the causes of the violence that threatens to exterminate them, they expend most of their energy convincing themselves that it does not really exist, that a reasonable solution will be found. This passive and unrealistic response to danger leaves the protagonists dead— just as it would leave thirty thousand Argentines dead in the next decade.

During this first period, the inchoate and "unreal" nature of Gambaro's onstage world led commentators (erroneously, though perhaps understandably) to compare Gambaro's early work with the theater of the absurd. From her first play onward, however, Gambaro rejects the absurdist separation of "art" (as an autonomous universe with its own laws and logic as conceived by Ionesco) and "reality." On the contrary, she calls attention to the interconnectedness of the two realms. They are by no means separate. While she does not explicitly refer to a concrete sociohistoric context in this stage of her career, she demonstrates how art reflects and constitutes reality. In turn, she emphasizes, art is often manipulated by those in power for real political aims. In *The Walls,* she juxtaposes her Young Man to an elegant painting of a young man. The painting of the young man vanishes as the room moves in on its inmate. Then the Young Man vanishes. During the next years thousands and thousands of Argentines would vanish. The painting reappears to lull the next victim into complacency. Art not only gives us insight into reality, but it can also be manipulated, and it plays a role in ongoing power struggles regardless of the artist's intent. Art is neither immune nor separate. It is precisely because the seemingly autonomous frames between the aesthetic and political are intricately connected that theaters in Argentina are bombed and theater practitioners are attacked or silenced. Yet the artificial "frame" (be it the ornate frame of the painting or the proscenium stage of the play) draws our attention away from this vital connection; it dissociates us from everything surrounding it. The separation proves not only untenable but also dangerous. By concealing the relation between the various systems of representation, the frame creates a perceptual blind spot that incapacitates the spectator from dealing with the larger picture. Framing does not protect the victims from harm; it does not keep serenity in and violence out. Gambaro urges the spectators to see beyond the seeming comfort and safety of the "magnificent carved frame" and the curtained room so that we can recognize the dangers that the frame apparently keeps out—the screams from the neighboring rooms/cells, the violent deaths, the facts of abduction and torture. We ignore them, as Argentines were soon to learn, at our peril.

Rather than place Gambaro's early dramatic production at the end of a literary tradition (the theater of the absurd), we must recognize that it is the beginning of a new discourse on fascism and atrocity. Gambaro, throughout her career, incessantly calls attention to the fascistic elements in Argentine government and discourse. Fascism has a long history in Argentina. In 1930 General Uriburu came to office with an agenda modeled on European fascism. Gambaro's portrayal of fascism, however, is also directed toward the present, explicitly expressing her alarm at the new wave of authoritarianism in Argentina and the country's ongoing, and intensifying, fascination with fascism.

In the early 1970s Gambaro pushes the "drama of disappearance" further. Her plays of this period, notably *Saying Yes* (*Decir sí,* 1972), *Strip* (*El despojamiento,* 1972) and *Information for Foreigners* (*Información para extranjeros,* 1973) eliminate any remaining vestiges of rationality or coherence from the onstage world. The Man in *Saying Yes* walks into the barbershop for a haircut, and the "inscrutable" Barber slits his throat. In the devastating play *Strip,* the Woman goes for an audition and spends the entire play in the waiting room, where she is gradually stripped of everything she has, down to and including her sense of self. She, like Emma before her, is deprecated for trying to cultivate what her sexist society promotes as an acceptable image for women. *Information* brings us even closer to the process of annihilation by guiding a real audience through a house in which acts of torture and murder are taking place in the halls and behind half-closed doors. The audience members, like Gambaro's protagonists before, are now the ones who see themselves stumbling into the wrong play. Gone are all recognizable frameworks or story lines, and by extension any basis, however tenuous, from which to explain or justify the crimes. There is no mistaken identity, no home to fight over (*Siamese Twins*), no jewelry or clothes left to steal (*The Blunder*). Gone is the characterization, exposition, complication, and "conflict" normally associated with drama. Instead of the two-act plays of the 1960s, Gambaro's plays of the 1970s are fragmented, very short one-acts like *Saying Yes* and *Strip,* or the episodic *Information,* "A Chronicle in Twenty Scenes." Precisely by not explaining, by not filling in the gaps, this is the drama of the "missing." Gambaro places the spectators in the naked contradiction of her historic moment, which now she makes perfectly explicit: "No one under eighteen will be admitted. Or under thirty-five or over thirty-six. . . . The play speaks to our way of life: Argentine, Western, and Christian. We are in 1971." Her pieces, like the historic moment producing them, challenge us to adapt to, ignore, or make sense of crazed contradiction.

In *Information,* the general audience becomes the focal point of the spectacle. Gambaro concentrates on a question she has posited, but only indirectly, in her theater of the 1960s: How can people deny what they know to be true? The audience is split up into groups upon arrival, each led through the house by a Guide introducing the various scenes with short excerpts about abductions and murders taken from actual contemporary newspapers. Again, and more explicitly, Gambaro challenges us to draw that fine line between the aesthetic and the political. The audience follows the Guide down long, dark passageways cluttered with corpses and prisoners, up and down steep, dangerous staircases, in and out of small rooms in which isolated acts of torture or theatrical rehearsals are forever being played out. The highlight of the tour is the visit to the catacombs in the basement, the tombs of martyred Christians. Although a member of the group (actually an actor) is attacked and abducted by unidentified men, the Guide encourages his group to overlook the violent intrusions. He dispels the rampant outbursts of violence as peripheral to the audience's right to entertainment. As screams and shouts resound through the corridors, he clamors for amusement and "a little gaiety, dammit!" and grumbles about the bad scripts and the unsavory subject matter. Complaining that "modern theater is like this! No respect for the ladies," he nonetheless encourages the spectators to enjoy the show. After all, he reminds us, we've paid for it.

As opposed to earlier plays in which Gambaro shows us that violence has erased the boundaries between the private and the public, between the inner and the outer, in *Information* she places the spectator in the very center of the collapsed and terrifying universe. *Information* actually stages that conflation by setting the violence in a house rather than a theater. Society as a whole, Gambaro stresses, has been transformed into a terrifying theatrical set, giving new meaning to the term *environmental theater.* Scenes of political violence are not limited to prisons and torture chambers but are played out on public streets, in private houses, on human bodies. The lines of demarcation between public and private having been wiped out, violence blurs all physical, moral, and judicial frameworks. Again, the takeover of the house, which is concurrently a social structure, the family home, and the body's protective shell, indicates that the three spaces—body, family, society—are all interconnected and all under attack. Terrorism in the home "gets us where we live," nullifying the existence of any safe space. No one is safe, and the Guide reminds his group to watch their step and their pocketbooks. The house reflects the invasive tactics of terrorism and torture. Terror deterritorializes; we are all foreigners in this house.

As spectators, we make our way through the dark passages,

peering through half-open doors, inadvertently entering the wrong room, and we see what we do not want to see, the non-aestheticized, noneroticized infliction of pain and violence on defenseless victims. Yet how can we distance ourselves from the reality we see with our own eyes? By turning it into theater. Gambaro's scenarios of torture demonstrate that theatrical inversion, distancing, and role-playing are essential for the continued functioning of torture. A young woman, totally despondent, dripping wet, and shivering in a chair, has just been submitted to the *submarino,* the prolonged submersion of the victim's head in water, an Argentine specialty. The visual image of the tortured, semiconscious woman is incongruent with the apparent benevolence of the scene, for the Guard acts as if he were her friend or lover trying to protect her. He molests her sexually even as he generously leaves his loaded pistol behind as a "favor" to her, just in case she wants to end it all. This may be hell, but the Guide is no Virgil; he too wants to molest the woman when he judges that no one is looking. In another room, the Milgram experiment is under way. The "pupil" is strapped to a chair and given electric shocks by the "teacher." Though the Pupil suffers from a weak heart, the experimenter urges the Teacher to increase the voltage. The experimenter posits the traditional arguments supporting torture: the experiment is necessary; it's for the greater social good; the man dialing up the lethal voltage is not responsible for the victim's death.

How can we deny what we know to be true? By listening to an expert telling us it's necessary, it's for our good, violence is not violence, it's really something else; by participating in a drama that inverts roles and changes names to create the illusion of innocence. The theatricality of the proceedings, on a practical level, admirably fulfills its real function. It makes us participate, either directly or indirectly, in annihilating acts from which we would rather distance ourselves.

The theatricality of torture, then, tries to makes violence "safe" for the audience. The audience feels it can remain on the sidelines. We can pretend we are neither directly involved nor responsible. One of the functions of theater, as articulated by theorists from Aristotle to Artaud, has always been to make violence safe for the audience. But it also converts people into a "safe" audience, one that will not interfere or disrupt the show. Terrorism atomizes and immobilizes the population; it transforms us from active players into a passive audience, content with sitting in our seats and "just watching." As the tour through this house illustrates, terrorism plays with potent images of darkness and the unknown. It capitalizes on infantile fantasies, fears of destruction, dismemberment, and suffocation. It works through amplification: a few displays of highly dramatic violence can hold hostage an entire society. The hideous intrusion of children's songs and games in the play illustrates how terrorism pushes the population to regress to those early areas of experience that prove most disempowering and hardest to decode. One approaches as an adult and turns away as a frightened child incapable of action. Moreover, the "fictions" offered by those in power allow spectators deniability. We didn't know what was happening. Thus, passivity can also be rationalized by means of the nightmarish mechanism of grotesque and dangerous inversion; the regime must be right. Maybe those victims were subversives; people don't disappear for no reason. The rationalization of the irrational brutality in turn becomes a tacit complicity, producing guilt. This group guilt ties the population to the criminal process, making it difficult for people to extricate themselves and condemn the proceedings.

Given that theater's illusionistic qualities can be used to incapacitate a population and preclude constructive participation, how can Gambaro hope to communicate the atrocious reality of terrorism and torture through theater? Her main response in plays like *Information* is to focus not only on the acts of violence themselves but also on the spectators watching them, on the act of watching. We turn our heads when we hear footsteps, crane our necks to catch a glimpse. The Guide's comments and suggestions constantly call attention to the fact that the spectators are "looking." The looking, not the violence, is central. The emphasis on our actions and reactions places us in the position of "seen object," normally reserved for the actors. This reversal implicates us in the action and calls attention to our role in violence. It strips us of our traditional invisibility as spectators.

In referring to *we,* the spectators, I do so consciously in order to emphasize that Gambaro forces us to relinquish our comforting assumptions about violence, our claims to deniability, innocence, and quietism. Instead, she urges us to analyze what prompts it, what makes it politically expedient, what makes it possible. But these questions are inextricable from an understanding of our role in it, either as voyeurs, disinterested bystanders, or victims. Whether we are physically involved in the performance or reading about the atrocities in the newspaper, whether we are Argentines trying to survive in an authoritarian system or foreign investors who want to ensure economic "stability," we participate in the brutality depicted here. As the title of *Information for Foreigners* makes clear, we are the spectators. This is our show. If we are not enjoying it (a possibility Gambaro foresees in the play itself), we might decide to pay attention to this information.

Gambaro's plays of the 1980s, among them *Royal Gambit* (*Real envido*, 1980), *Bitter Blood* (*La malasangre*, 1981), *From the Rising Sun* (*Del sol naciente*, 1983), and *Antígona Furiosa* (1986), continue to examine the victimizer-victim relationship, but with important differences that reflect Argentina's changing sociopolitical climate. The victims have finally differentiated themselves from their oppressors. While they remain powerless in the face of the absolute brutality and stupidity of authority figures, they no longer deceive themselves about what is happening to them. The victims have moved from the passive acceptance of catastrophe in the early plays to an acute awareness that their passivity has contributed to their own annihilation. Now the victims, especially the women like Dolores, Suki, Ama, and Antígona, denounce authority for all the world to hear; they scream out against atrocity during their victimizations and after their deaths. Much as in the case of the "disappeared," the dead voices of these victims cannot be silenced. They are felt not as absence but as presence.

Though the victims no longer participate in the fictionalization of reality, the fictions themselves keep proliferating, suggesting the elaborate process of legitimation necessary to keep the criminal authorities in power. The authority figures behind the crumbling sociopolitical realms portrayed in these plays (personified by the King in *Royal Gambit*, the Father in *Bitter Blood*, Oban in *From the Rising Sun*, and Creon in *Antígona Furiosa*) attempt to mask the economic and moral bankruptcy of their regimes. They try to inscribe the vacuum left by the multiple disappearances with some socially acceptable meaning.

While the theater of this period continues to depict the effects of social crisis, Gambaro's main concern lies in dismantling the fictions of power devised to justify and normalize the abusiveness of those in control. The problem, as Dolores makes clear in *Bitter Blood,* is that the interests of the rulers blatantly go against the general good. In order to maintain and consolidate power, as the four successive military juntas between 1976 and 1983 indicate, rulers have to come up with new arguments to justify their crimes. Failing to justify their position on the rhetorical grounds of "national security" and "economic stability"—both suspect now that the authorities can ensure neither—the question becomes how to divert public attention from the pitiful, dead-end situation in which people (on- and offstage) find themselves. Terror and crisis, leaders know, can disorient and, for a time, immobilize a population. War, of course, has often functioned as a national diversion. Engaging in war proves a successful strategy, or gambit, at least temporarily, for the military men in *Royal Gambit* and *From the Rising Sun,* much as it did for the Argentine generals in the Falklands, or Malvinas. But in Gambaro's plays, much as in Argentina in 1983, the victimized population has disengaged from the fictions of potency and grandeur. Now it recognizes the price it has paid, and has yet to pay, for going along with the party line. As Suki laments in *From the Rising Sun,* the military "told us it was necessary. Those things happen in war. People . . . die. They . . . want us to keep quiet." Ama, in the same play, reproaches herself and her countrymen that no one dared face the reality of the warrior caste: "They marched before a congregation of blind men! No one dared look at them!"

Antígona Furiosa, written after the end of the Dirty War, illustrates Gambaro's technique of being politically pertinent, even urgent, while maintaining the semblance of so-called universal appeal. *Antígona* is both a retelling of the Sophoclean tragedy and, on another level, a dramatization of the struggle by the Mothers of the Plaza de Mayo to recover their children's corpses— which at least in the early period of the Mothers' activity was one of the principal goals. Estela de Carlotto, one of the Mothers, recounts how in 1977 she pleaded with General Bignone (who became junta leader in 1982) to release her daughter Laura: "He said they didn't want to have prisons full of 'subversives,' as he called them . . . that they had to do what was necessary, by which it was clear he meant to kill them. I was now certain that Laura was dead so I asked please, would he at least return the body because I didn't want to search cemeteries amongst the anonymous graves for the body of my daughter."[3]

Gambaro's *Antígona* begins where Sophocles's play ends, with Antígona hanging with a noose around her neck. After a moment, however, she takes the noose off, arranges her dress, and begins the play. The image of Antígona hanging both ties the play directly into the Sophoclean model and marks its departure from it, signaling the direction that Gambaro will take. Antígona, like the Mothers, is intent on burying her dead, even though Creon has forbidden it. Antígona, like the Mothers, renounces the traditional sphere of home and married life (represented by Haemon) and takes to the streets, even though it is forbidden to protest or associate with others: "Antígona walks among her dead, in a strange gait in which she falls and recovers, falls and recovers." Polynices, like the disappeared, remains unmourned and unburied. Creon, the voice of authority emanating from an empty shell, orders that he remain so. His command "Let no one come near—dare—to come near, like the mad girl circling, circling the unburied unburied unburied corpse" recalls the Mothers' weekly march around the Plaza de Mayo, demanding justice for their children. They too were called madwomen, "las locas de la Plaza de Mayo." Antígona, like the Mothers, carries her dead *with* her and *on* her in her own flesh. The Mothers used placards with the names and photographs of their missing children, speaking in their names. In like fashion Antígona promises her brother that she will be his breath, his mouth, his legs, his feet: "The living are the great sepulchre of the dead."

The Chorus, depicted as two *porteños* (i.e., from Buenos Aires) drinking coffee in a café, are complicit with Creon's criminal abuse of power. They accept Creon's prohibitions as normative, and thus, they deem it logical that citizens will comply with them: "No fool is fool as far as loving death." They, like other Gambaro characters before, participate in the official silencing and the negation of reality. They echo the values handed down by the junta: "Who holds a loved one dearer than his country is despicable." Or: "Anarchy is the worst blow . . . I trust only those who are obedient." Or: "Punishment always presupposes crime, my girl. There are no innocents. . . . if punishment comes down on you, you did something you shouldn't have done."

Antígona, unlike Gambaro's characters of the 1960s and 1970s, refuses to be silenced by the voice of authority. She explicitly challenges the authoritarian decrees and denies them legitimacy: Creon, she observes, "thinks the law is law because it comes out of his mouth." If she is pronounced a madwoman for demanding justice for her dead, then those who denounce her are crazy. What values or attributes could possibly legitimate such a regime? Like many others who contradicted or opposed the military's mono-lithic monologue in Argentina, however, Antígona also disap-pears. She, like many Argentine victims, is a "future corpse," the name given by the military to victims who were destroyed alive, either flung out of airplanes or buried: "Let the laws, these vile laws! drag me to a cave that will be my tomb. No one will hear my weeping; no one will be aware of my suffering. They will live in the light as though nothing were happening. . . . I will be . . . uncounted among the living and among the dead. I will disappear from the world, alive." And as in the original Sophoclean tragedy, Antígona hangs herself rather than endure this end.

The last image of *Antígona* is the same as the first: Antígona hangs herself. The act temporarily closes the circle of violence, a circle that bespeaks not only the Mothers' endless quest for justice but also the circular, repetitive, seemingly endless manifestations of violence itself. Antígona's death at the end of the play, echoing the first scene, suggests that this "end" is only a pause. The disap-peared are not dead and buried. Order and harmony have not been restored. In spite of President Alfonsin's and President Menem's desire to put Argentina's tragedy behind them, there is no *Punto Final* or final closing point. The drama of oppression and defiance is not over.

During thirty years, in which Gambaro has written as many plays, her onstage worlds reflect the evolving consciousness of crisis, from the initial experience of social collapse to the critical understanding of how and why crisis becomes cemented into the disintegrating social fabric. Continual crisis in Argentina has jus-tified the existence of an active military; it has made necessary ever-escalating acts of social control. Even now in the early 1990s, the military forces loom just behind the scene. As one of the outgoing generals warned a journalist in 1983: "Don't do anything silly, because this is a country where history changes back and forth like a pendulum. And it always repeats itself."[4] As Gam-baro's plays make clear, Argentina's tragedy is far from over. As always with Griselda Gambaro's work, it behooves us to listen.

Diana Taylor

Notes

1. David Rock, *Argentina, 1516–1987* (Berkeley: University of California Press, 1987), 347, 349.

2. Diana Taylor, *Theatre of Crisis: Drama and Politics in Latin America* (Lexington: University Press of Kentucky, 1991).

3. Jo Fisher, *Mothers of the Disappeared* (Boston: South End Press, 1989), 20.

4. John Simpson and Jana Bennett, *The Disappeared and the Mothers of the Plaza* (New York: St. Martin's Press, 1985), 30.

Library of Congress Cataloging-in-Publication Data

Gambaro, Griselda.
    [Plays. English. Selections]
    Information for foreigners : three plays / by Griselda Gambaro ;
edited, translated, and with an introduction by Marguerite
Feitlowitz ; with an afterword by Diana Taylor.
        p.   cm.
    Translation of: Las paredes, Información para extranjeros, and
Antigona Furiosa.
    ISBN 0-8101-1008-3 (cloth : alk. paper). — ISBN 0-8101-1033-4
(paper : alk. paper)
    1. Gambaro, Griselda—Translations into English.   I. Feitlowitz,
Marguerite.   II. Title.
PQ7797.G253A19   1992
862—dc20   91-33215
                                                               CIP